Bound

For Rachel —
Best Wishes,
Ji M

BOUND

JAMES McKEAN

Contemporary Nonfiction

Truman State University Press
Kirksville, Missouri

Cover art: McKean family photo, ca. 1950. Used courtesy of author.
Cover design: Lisa Ahrens

Library of Congress Cataloging-in-Publication Data

Names: McKean, James, 1946 July 4– author.
Title: Bound / by James McKean.
Description: Kirksville, MO : Truman State University Press, [2017] |
    Series: Contemporary nonfiction
Identifiers: LCCN 2017008917| ISBN 9781612482026 (softcover :
    acid-free paper) | ISBN 9781612482033 (ebook)
Subjects: LCSH: McKean, James, 1946 July 4—Family. | Authors,
    American—20th century—Biography. | Families—United States—
    Anecdotes.
Classification: LCC PS3563.C3737 Z46 2017 | DDC 813/.54 [B] —dc23
    LC record available at https://lccn.loc.gov/2017008917

The paper in this publication meets or exceeds the minimum requirements of the American National Standard for Information Sciences—
Permanence of Paper for Printed Library Materials, ANSI Z39.48–1992.

For Simon

Contents

Acknowledgments

Grateful acknowledgment is made to the editors of the following journals in which versions of these essays first appeared:

"Posting" in *Briar Cliff Review* (Spring 2013); "Lesson Plan" in *Cold Mountain Review* (Fall 2013); "Rootie Kazoo-tie One-Man Band" and "Handwork" in *Gettysburg Review* (Winter 2008 and Autumn 2015) reprinted here with the acknowledgment of the editors; "Bound" in *Iowa Review* (Spring 2007); "Let Me Be Richard" in *Southern Review* (Summer 2015); "So Much More" in *Southern Humanities Review* (Spring 2013); "Dyed-in-the-Wool" in *Tampa Review* (Fall 2011).

My thanks to the good people at Truman State University Press, and to friends who gave their time and attention to these essays: Charlie Drum, William Ford, Jim Grove, Cassie Kircher, Vicky Maloy, Keith Ratzlaff, and Len Sandler. I'm especially grateful to Patricia Foster, Robert Grunst, and Paul Zimmer, fine teachers and writers who read these essays with care and concern and affection. As I have said before, their encouragement, good sense, critical insight, and friendship have sustained me for many years.

Finally, my thanks and love to our daughter, Meryl, and to my wife, Penny, who has always been my best reader.

Introduction

My need to revisit the women in my life starts with my mother. She left us slowly before we lost her—a pernicious crumbling that began in 2001 when she took her first trip to New York City, an eighty-three-year-old widow on a tour with her Shrine lady friends from Tacoma, Washington. As fate would have it, at nine in the morning on September 11, 2001, she was on a charter bus working its way through Manhattan's streets toward Pier 83. When I finally reached her by phone late that afternoon, she was back in her downtown hotel, locked down in effect. They just turned the bus around, she said. She sounded frightened and disoriented—no wonder, the whole city in turmoil. The whole country.

What she didn't tell me then on the phone was that she had fallen in the hotel's bathroom, the first of many falls over the next few years as she grew more confused and the bills and dishes piled up around her. My mother always feared she would suffer the same fate as her mother, and she did. For five years my mother slipped away in the care of my brother, her favorite son, whom she would forget as well. Alzheimer's, the doctor penciled in as the cause of death, an illness we had suspected but refused to acknowledge.

No one was talking. Not talking seems to be our family's way. Reticence, accounts held close to the vest, mum's the word, lives and histories "not for you," my grandmother said to me on more than one occasion. For years that had to serve. When I was growing up, the women in my family—aunts, grandmothers, my mother—set the domestic stage with their productions: food, caretaking, the house tidy and secure. Deaf to them, if they spoke to me much at all, I ran headlong out the back door each morning and returned pitch-stained for dinner, my attention still tree-bound in the woods of Hamlin Park. I assumed meals would grace our table forever.

"What did I know, what did I know?" Robert Hayden asks of his indifferent boyish self when he remembers how his father cared for him. Let me admit the same for the women who shaped my world from the contour of my feet to the haircut above my clean collar. They weren't looking, I thought, as I escaped, trying to find myself. They spent their days industrious and fretful, both independent and dutiful, busy dawn to dusk setting the schedule and the limits wherein I ran my heedless ways. They kept house, kept up with their lives and jobs, kept an eye on me.

What I didn't know as a boy was legion. Perhaps they preferred it that way. My wife, on the other hand, has spent the last forty-two years turning my gaze from childish things. She adopted my family as I did hers, mothers-in-law and grandmothers to discover. Then our daughter stood center stage, her growing up as baffling in its complications as the clouds. "Oh, Dad," she would say, her grimace suggesting I was hopeless, my questions all trespass. Where did such weather come from, we'd ask ourselves? Now she has a son. It's his turn to run headlong into the sun-filled days. Such is the universe. Left behind, I wish my mother could have seen him. In my daughter's voice calling after her boy, I hear her mother. In my daughter's worry I remember my own mother up late at night and smoking, the windows dark and bills laid out on her kitchen table. My mother died in 2008. The more I imagine her over time, the closer she draws.

In "Toward a Definition of Creative Nonfiction," Bret Lott says we write with a "desire not to let slip altogether away our lives as we have known them, and to put an order—again for better or worse—to our days." I write about these women from memory and research and imagination—these remarkable women who precede my daughter. Aware of how to survive their time and place, each fashioned a life for herself: a great-great-grandmother who found the wherewithal to divorce her abusive husband in 1860 in Wisconsin, after thirty years of marriage and eight children. A "new woman" who rode the train alone from Boston at the turn of the twentieth century, a .41 caliber derringer in her purse, to look for work in Washington State. Her daughter, my aunt, who swam for the Washington Athletic Club, held a number of world records and won a bronze medal in the 1936 Olympics in Berlin. And my wife's grandmother, once "Queen for a Day," who pulled up stakes and moved for the sake of a little girl.

And let me admit that by writing about them, I may have turned the light of betrayal on what they wished left in shadow, the enigmatic, the nuances of their internal lives, restrained or hidden by gender and class. I can only imagine their lives. They are real people. For years, I have been away. To write and revise is to see them again. To write about their lives is to write about my own life as well. Vivian Gornick explains, such is "the betrayal of intimacy necessary to the act of becoming oneself."

One morning long ago, I left home. Now hearing my name called across the neighborhood at dusk, I look for a way back. Dead reckoning perhaps, I find myself in good company.

Lesson Plan

Plan for the class to be over. But in the meantime, week after week, move closer, for she sits always to one side of the classroom near the window, the same chair. She will be the first to take the papers, instructions, announcements you have duplicated for them all, and she will take one and pass the rest. Be amazed why this is special. Move toward her one half a chair length per week. Arrive before she does, and nod and say hello, for she is lovely and composed, an off-white blouse, a sleeveless sweater, jeans, her blond hair tied back. She has blue-gray eyes when you look closely, trying not to dwell, saying thank you and how are you and hope your weekend went well, this Monday of the tenth week of class, a room full of eccentrically good students, a retired physician from the state penitentiary, the housewife novelist and fan of e. e. cummings, the grocer, the Vietnam vet.

Every day you are taken first by how she looks, upright, ankles crossed, but every day it's her timing that amazes, for she has saved you on more than one occasion, the talkers in this class gifted and spontaneous and when the conversation stalls or meanders, she raises her hand. *Would it help to find a central metaphor?* she might ask, brow furrowed, a question she must know leads you to an answer you know, that settles the air back onto the poem at hand. She listens and nods. Finally, it's her writing all these weeks that has won you over late at night in lamplight when you hear her voice and understand maybe a little how she composes her world in simple vignettes. Here in clean, precise prose she rides in the backseat of her parents' car, wondering through the rain-streaked window what might become of her on some other road on some other evening.

When you hold the semester's last conference at a table in the cafeteria, announced in the syllabus, she will arrive on time and you will lose your train of thought, margin notes forgotten. Careful. And when you blurt out, "Who are you? I'd really like to know," she looks caught in the rain. No, no. Too personal. Foolish. Better to have addressed her work and what she likes to read, *The Lord of the Rings* you will find out later and large classics and mysteries started in the middle. Here is a moment to recover. "Sorry, that was out of line," you might say but she will not forget over these next forty minutes what you have asked, and maybe she wonders herself why in this class unlike any other she has felt so inclined to speak out, has offered her opinion about poems and stories, what feels genuine and moving, what seems true. And now the rain falls.

Am I careless? she might question as well. Hadn't she been warned by her overbearing family beneath a roof of narrow tolerances, the dinner candles starved in the thin, critical air? Danger. But both of you, student and instructor, know the conversation has changed. She gathers her books and notebook and must leave for work, she says, and sorry the semester is over and thank you, a formality you return, saying how you have enjoyed having her in class and so admired her work and hope to see her again, a simple courtesy these words, she may think, that drift after her and dissipate in the afternoon air. But you know what you mean. You want to see more of her, to draw closer, and have no idea how to do this now the artifice of the class has expired. She is twenty, and you are twenty-six and stumped.

Your roommate Brian suggests an intermediary. You live in a dump—three horse-kicked acres, a two-bedroom house furnished with wire spools, boxes, palooka couches, folding chairs, and two German shepherds, one classically saddled and kind, the other blond and murderous. "I think a friend of mine Julie knows her," your roommate offers. "She can ask whether your fair student would go out with you. By the way, aren't there rules about this sort of thing?"

"The class is over," you say, not sure about what's acceptable at this small college, the precedents if any, the ethics, the application of the term "moral turpitude," printed in boldface across your contract like a prophecy to firing. Lose the contract. Don't ask.

"Julie will talk to her and let you know, and maybe the four of us could head for the Blue Mountains to cut a Christmas tree."

You wait. His friend Julie doesn't call. You don't have her phone number, but you do have your student's number retrieved from the registrar's office for "business" purposes. It is December 15, and the class has been over for a week. Still no word. "Did she find out?" you ask your roommate.

"Got me," he says, oblivious to your pacing back and forth before the phone.

The next step must be anti-Prufrockian. Time is running out along with your patience. If you call first, will she think you're too forward? She wished the semester longer, no? Or will she say, "That's not what I meant. That's not what I meant at all."

OK. It's time to dial, number by number. It doesn't matter that your roommate's friend had called and asked your good student what she thought about the possibility of going out with you, her instructor, maybe something simple like coffee or a show, the conventional no more no less. And what you don't need to know is that your good student had said absolutely not, that's not done, I couldn't think of it. What a horrifying prospect.

The problem, or maybe your good fortune, is that Julie didn't relay any of this to you, and now the phone is ringing, and your student's mother answers. When you introduce yourself, she says yes as if she knows who you are. You ask to speak to Penny, for that is your good student's name. She must be standing close by because she answers at once.

"Remember me?" you ask, though it's lame you realize. "How are things?"

"I'm glad the semester's over [*oh, no*]. You?"

"Fine. Thanks. Still finishing up, you know, papers and things. But I was wondering [*here we go*] this Friday if you'd like to go with us to cut a Christmas tree in the Blue Mountains, you know, just outside of Walla Walla, maybe for the afternoon, a couple of hours in the afternoon? Back by five."

"Well . . . [*Interminable wait. Ear buzz and rush. Oh, to be deferential now, useful, a bit obtuse*] . . . sure."

"Yes? Terrific." You're pleased, though baffled. How can you lose three quarters of your vocabulary in a thirty-second conversation? Don't worry. The words will come back. You will need them.

◌   ◌   ◌

The vehicle will be a 1962 Volkswagen Bus, a twenty-three window, red and white Samba, with forty-one brake horsepower, three OK tires and the spare. Your roommate drives and you hold a piece of paper with directions to find your student, her family's house west of Pasco at the end of a long driveway.

One complication. It's snowing, not a blizzard but steady. Unusual for this time in this country, big flakes cover the streets and the yards and the driveway that Brian tries to negotiate, unsure now of the boundaries. Her house lies up ahead, but how to get there? Where to park? The snow covers everything. Do you turn left or right at the house? Although it's early in your lesson plan, where you park yourself is crucial. You'll be given a chance to retake this quiz, but today your roommate decides to try circumnavigation. Oh, what they must have seen from inside—a Volkswagen Bus with two mustached guys, hair sticking out from their stocking caps, puttering by the front door, the side bedrooms, the master bedroom, the patio in front of the living room, the breakfast nook, the kitchen, and finally skidding so slightly before the garage door they missed on their first time around. You have arrived.

Penny is out the back door fast. It will be some time before she tells you that her father's favorite pastime is tending his four acres of lawn you have driven slowly across. Today she smiles. Someone waves from the door. When you slide open the Bus door, you extend your hand. She takes it and steps up to sit beside you, and from then on—the Bus accelerating first to Julie's house and then south toward the Blue Mountains—the gears shift. The beginning is silence and small talk and snow outside the window and portends nothing of the complications you will discover in this relationship and what you will be asked and how moment-by-moment will unfold in the community of her family. Your future will study a new history, albums and narratives, the mythologies of Norway, Wisconsin, and North Dakota. Count on daily phone calls. Soon enough there will be tribunals of aunts and dinner each Sunday, and awkward silences when the family gathers on the Fourth to eat potato salad and burned dogs. Fireworks. Camping trips with friends. Movies and walks and letters when you part for more than a day. Long weekend trips to Tacoma. Fishing at Westport. Vancouver B.C.

museums and walks through old-growth forests. Brothers and cousins and sisters and their children. And then six months later she will move away to attend another school and you will take a leave from teaching, by coincidence, to attend the same school. You will spend a year together, walking to class and back, shopping, cooking meals and sitting at a small rented table in a small apartment. A year for study and living.

But this is all yet to come, your asking her beneath the Narrows Bridge in Tacoma to marry you, and her saying yes, and how she will insist on being married at home in Pasco. How you will buy a green-checked, bell-bottomed suit for this very occasion, your fashion sense outdone only by your best man's blue-checked sports coat, blue pants, and white bucks, this being 1974. You will never have more hair than on that day, sunny and bright with champagne and good wishes, many friends having traveled a long way to wish you well and honor your parents, who stand in the receiving line as if blessed.

But not yet. The Christmas tree in the Blue Mountains lies ahead. From the Forest Service, you have purchased one red-tag tree permit, pine or fir. You would like her to choose, and when you reach the national forest, the Bus parked, having slid into a ditch, you and Penny walk, lunches packed in your backpack, a thermos of tea, the snow ankle deep. This one? Or that? Too thin. Too short. Who can decide? Tree after tree, green and fragrant in the falling snow, the elevation enough to fog her breathing as you walk behind her up a slight incline, the Volkswagen in sight back down the hill. Her parka is blue and her knit hat gray with red striping. She turns and asks if you have decided just as you reach down to cup a handful of snow and pack it hand over hand.

She says "Oh, no," and reaches down into the snow herself only to slip both feet out and land rear first. There she is sitting in the snow, Penny, you standing over her, watching, snowball in hand, frozen a moment. Her cheeks are red in the cold air, her hair still tucked beneath her cap. She is not smiling and leans on one hand, the semester over finally, and lifts the other toward you and says, "This is where you help me up."

Yes. Of course. And you extend your hand, unaware at that moment there will be no other future for you besides her, thinking only that she is no longer your student, that you have much to learn, that you will need to find a new vocabulary for her and you and that may take forever. Take stock of yourself and invent and prepare. Start with the tree. A fir you both agree is gorgeous, taller than she and shorter than you, the branches full around. You cut it with a hand saw, the pitch redolent, and bind the tree with cords, sanction it with a red tag, and tie it on top of the Bus, which you both help push out of the ditch, the engine whining, the tires spinning and catching on the road back. Then it's a cup of wine shared between you all and the radio playing as the evening settles in early this short day in December, the air warm inside the Bus as she removes her cap and leans her head, sleepy on your shoulder.

Not far now. You will put your arm around her and rest your cheek against the top of her head. She smells like mountain air, pine and cedar, and when you kiss her forehead once, she settles in, her cap in hand all the way home, where her father, in Penny's afternoon absence, has lined the driveway with pylons (his firewood) on both sides clear to the back door that stands open now. He will wait there to look you up and down and shake your hand for the first time.

Rootie Kazootie
One-Man Band

I'm waiting in Lane 2 for the Mukilteo ferry. One passenger and vehicle, nine dollars. Thirty steaming minutes to Clinton on Whidbey Island, then a twenty-minute drive to Keystone where I'll catch another ferry to Port Townsend. By lunchtime, I should be in Sequim, Washington, where my mother, unhappy, is expecting me.

When I was young, impatient and afraid at the same time, I hated this wait for the ferry and then hated the ferry butting into pilings, its bulk and churning, and then the ferry's whistle splitting Mukilteo up the white line of its one road. I hid in the backseat of my father's '54 Mercury and covered my ears.

Today, the wait is fortuitous and nostalgic. Maybe at fifty-eight I'm less anxious to get to where I'm supposed to go. Or maybe I'm dragging my feet again as I did at dusk years ago outside our house, my mother's voice having echoed through the woods, calling me home to explain myself before dinner. Now, in a role reversal, I've traveled from Iowa City to explain to my mother, who is eighty-five, why she should no longer drive, why assisted living serves her needs far better than her living alone, and what she might do with a few of her things, especially her organ, in disrepair (too many silent keys) and too large for her new apartment. After 1,500 miles I will walk through the door to say hello, and she will ask why I haven't visited more often. Well, what did I expect?

I walk down to Mukilteo's public beach, next to its historic lighthouse, and then back out onto the ferry landing to smell the salt air and creosote. Seagulls brood on the top of pilings; anemones and barnacles congregate at their roots. These are the same red and yellow anemones, the same barnacles, the same raucous gulls I heard when I finally exited the backseat of my father's car and followed him into Losvar's boathouse next to the ferry landing. We were on our way to Hat Island for the long Fourth of July weekend. Inside the dark gasoline-soaked air of the boathouse, my father and John Carlson uncovered John's eighteen-foot Mukilteo boat on its dolly, while I twisted the handle of my father's silent blue Evinrude.

Drifting back, I am maybe eight. My mother waits in the car, window open, as John and my father tow the boat by hand toward the light of the door. She wears a blue scarf, the knot tied beneath her chin. Her rain jacket unzipped, she smokes next to bags of groceries. Weeping, the block ice my father bought sits wrapped in burlap beside the car. She's waiting for the men to position the boat in the winch straps that will lift it onto the big trolley on rails.

In salt air, rust coats anything iron or steel except the tops of the well-used rails diving into the Sound. The trolley's winches and drums and steel ropes and grease-slick gears fascinate me, and when I reach for the teeth, my mother calls out to me. She's watching me and sounds perturbed. I pull my hand back, not sure exactly what I've done, though my stomach starts to ache.

I remember such an ache at home and wanting to escape each morning into the pine smell of Hamlin Park, or back to the Sound off Hat Island where the coho's silver flashes in green water, and fifteen-pound monofilament creases my hand as I pay out line into the waves.

At home the bristling, mysterious air flabbergasted me. I never knew what to expect. Neither my staying outside nor putting my nose in a book relieved the tension, the feeling that something was amiss. Sometimes in the late afternoon, I could sneak by when my mother sat at her organ to play "Happy Days Are Here Again" or "Blue Moon." Around a corner or down the hall, I would listen as she found her way through a song and then played it again without a stumble. This after her morning of washed floors. Sheets boiled. Flour and salt measured and mixed into a pot of chicken. She set the table and vacuumed and made beds and adjusted the pillows. She swept and polished. "Move your feet," she would say as if where I stood seemed always in question. If I ever stood still.

Naturally, I thought the problem lay with me. I thought if I could explain myself, maybe the air would lie still. Who are you? her demeanor seemed to ask, but I didn't know, and wandered the backyards and woods and rode great distances on my one-gear Schwinn to find out. Or I looked in books. *Captain Hornblower*, *A Connecticut Yankee in King Arthur's Court*, *The Sword and the Stone*, and *Gulliver's Travels* held me fast. Each was a search and an adventure, and in the end, a going home. Each articulated my day, morning to dusk, sailing or flying or riding in my daily search for treasure or names. When I was very young, I remember listening to Eddy Arnold sing on the radio as he spelled out a word, each letter standing for something special—a million things given, and what we owed, a tear and a heart of gold, loving eyes and what was right. I was so curious. What was the word? Once I heard it, I knew something in my life would be settled. Then he sang, "Put them all together they spell mother / A word that means the world to me."

I turned the radio off. The word "mother" felt less wonderful than urgent, more mysterious and unpredictable and difficult to please. I was at a loss for words around her, and words were important to me. I remember on our car trips to Portland asking my father to name the towns along the way, Olympia, for example, and Chehalis, where he was born, or Longview. Over and over, I asked the names of the places in between the towns, the fields, the green banks of fir trees and cedars, until my mother finally offered me a dime if I would keep silent for ten minutes. A penny a minute.

"I'm not sure these places have names," my father finally said to break the silence. This was an uncomfortable thought for me, all these nameless, blank spaces, as if names might pin the world down to keep it safe and stable.

Enigmatic, my mother seemed caught between names, especially those mornings she rolled her sleeves, scarf wound around her hair like a turban, a mop bucket and jars of floor wax laid out on the kitchen counter. She held the back door open and said, "Go." To Sunday school six blocks away—though sometimes I never made it past Our Lady of the Woods Next Door—to the ball field to play work-up or five hundred, or on my bike to as far as time would let me go halfway through the day before I turned back home. Fishing rod tied to the handlebars, bait and reel in the basket, my legs burning as I rode home one day from Lake Washington, the one cutthroat trout I snagged in a culvert beneath a back road stuffed in my pocket—an offering for her table. And once to Hamlin Park to climb the tallest tree I could find, a white pine one hundred feet high from which I could see clear back to our house on 171st Street, the madronas, the rock walls, the sun squinting and red in her ammonia-bright front window.

"You weren't getting into trouble, were you?" she would ask as I walked in the door. Even on the most innocent days, I felt as if I had found trouble. Her cross-examinations conflated statement and question, a way of giving and taking away, a way of hanging the laundry out to dry. Explain yourself, she meant to say, and I spent a considerable amount of time trying to figure out just how to do that. And still do. What kid knows who he or she is? It's as if I were a blank slate onto which each day's coincidences, the near misses, the vagaries, the smells and sunlight, the very trees, all pitch and needles, impressed themselves. My responses to the world were visceral, instincts sharpened in the woods or on the ball field. I was curious about what I didn't know and afraid of the big kids, my own imagination, or going home to what Robert Hayden calls "the chronic angers of that house." I waited all week for Saturday morning when the Ridgecrest Theater finally opened its doors.

Saturday meant double-feature matinees. Cheeks stuffed, popcorn in hand, the Ridgecrest crowd prepared for the worst. *The War of the Worlds.* When the lids screwed off the top of those house-sized meteors and the cobra-like head snaked around with a little TV in its mouth, I couldn't breathe. I pulled my jacket over my head and looked through the sleeve, *ping ping ping* as that Martian heat ray charred the dumbstruck, white-flag-waving onlooker like a hot dog on my dad's barbecue. Or worse, the Id monster in *Forbidden Planet.* It was invisible and as awful as my mind could conjure: fanged, huge, and malevolent. And then I saw *Invasion of the Body Snatchers.* If you can't find the enemy outside, then start looking inside, an Americanized form of self-persecution and paranoia boiling up since 1695.

◊ ◊ ◊

But what I really waited for during those Saturday matinees was the drawing. Here good luck might help me with my mother. She loved music. My father and she had purchased a small electric organ for our living room, and she polished its wood until my face beamed in the reflection. Sometimes when she played in the evening, I would lie quietly on the floor beside her organ and peer into its backside to watch the vacuum tubes pulse with light and volume. Maybe my playing music would catch her ear. So when the house lights came up after the feature and before the Buck Rogers serial, the theater manager walked up on stage and tugged at his bow tie, and I dug into my pocket for my ticket stub. Every so often that summer when I was eleven, the Ridgecrest Theater gave away a Rootie Kazootie One-Man Band, made famous by Sheriff Tex on Channel Five. More than once, some lucky kid returned from the stage with his arms around the cardboard box, grin blazing. I longed for a Rootie Kazootie One-Man Band. How I would express myself! How I would catch my mother's ear. Washboard upright in its stand, topped with two bulb horns, cymbal strapped to each knee, I would accompany myself with the deluxe Sheriff Tex raspberry kazoo. Scrape and bang, washboard and cymbal, foot stomping and a honk for emphasis. This would be my theme song, and I too would be blessed.

Alas, the one Saturday I remember, there was no band to be won. The theater manager held up a Mattel burp gun, capable of firing a whole roll of caps, then several ersatz Winchester lever-action popguns, with realistic, compressed air report, and called the first number. Not mine. Second number, no. Then before the third, the manager reached toward the back of his table to retrieve a large box. For a moment, I thought this might be my sought-after One-Man Band. But he said, "Now we have a prize for a girl," and he took a doll out of the box and held it up. I dropped my ticket into my lap, waiting. I could go for the popgun, or maybe the cap-firing burp gun that grew more attractive the more I thought about it. A whole roll of caps shot on one wind-up. That would roust the dogs. Then with great emphasis and suspense, the manager read my number.

I didn't realize this at first and looked around. Not a girl moved. Then I looked at my ticket, and he read my number off again. I stared at my ticket, frozen. "Has anybody got this number?" the manager asked again, raising his voice and scanning the theater.

"I've got it," I yelled from the back, an obedient student always and lifted the ticket up as if he could see it.

"Well, come down."

"I can't."

"Why not?"

"I'm not a girl." All gum chewing stopped. Laughter bubbled up as rows of heads turned.

"It doesn't matter. Come down. Pick another prize." Wishing I could crawl into my hat, I walked down the aisle, up the steps, head down, and selected my Winchester popgun. Careful not to fall off the stage, or trip back up the aisle, I made my escape without further incident through the lobby and out the door. How could good luck be so complicated?

◊ ◌ ◊

Convinced that I had exhausted my luck at the Ridgecrest Theater, I decided that afternoon to make my own Rootie Kazootie One-Man Band, improvising with pie plates taped to my knees, a tin bucket to kick, a tissue-paper kazoo, and a corrugated piece of fiberglass onto which I screwed my bike horn and bell. If only Sheriff Tex could have heard me that afternoon, scraping and honking beside the television, until my mother had had enough. From the kitchen she yelled, "Why don't you take that noise outside?" I knew it wasn't a real question.

A month later during sixth-grade flag football season and the wonderful backyard fall evenings in Seattle, my mother decided I needed music lessons. I don't remember her ever offering to teach me how to play her organ. Maybe I showed little interest beyond the racket of my One-Man Band. Maybe her sitting on the bench before those keys served as a place of refuge from such chaos. And in my mother's social construct, teaching was a job for school. That's why we parked and marched into Hamlin Park Elementary, navy-barracks-turned-elementary school, one Tuesday evening, found Mrs. Fustis, the band teacher, who took one look at me, all gangly and unsure, and pronounced that with such long arms, I was an ideal trombone player.

Even then I knew we'd been sold. What kid would choose a trombone? A trumpet, the shortstop of instruments, sure, where you could lead with high notes like Louis Armstrong, or even a clarinet like Benny Goodman's on the heavy 78s my mother played on the hi-fi. Those instruments were flashy and compact, and for a skinny eleven-year-old in a neighborhood full of sleeve-rolled, Vitalis-haired, Camel-smoking greasers, mobility was essential. Then somewhere behind the scenes, out of earshot, Mrs. Fustis convinced my mother that I should have a new trombone and case and music stand. Gold and glistening, the horn smelled of spit and metal and oil.

Thus began a winter's worth of trombone practice. At my best moments, I could work the slide, the notes oiled one to the other, and figure my way through "My Darling Clementine." In its case, however, the trombone felt like an anchor. Folding my music stand back up proved only slightly less difficult than riding the school bus home late in the early Seattle dark. After maneuvering up the bus steps, down the knee-hazard and toe-trap aisles and finally into the narrow seat next to Billy Jenkins, who smelled like tuna fish, I wedged myself in with my book bag, lunch box, and brown vinyl trombone case. I felt like a traffic jam. At each stop, a line of grumbling lunch boxes detoured around me and out the door, but I tried to ignore them until my stop loomed up, the bus clanked to a halt, the driver winched open the door, and I crabbed my way into the night.

◊   ◊   ◊

The Mukilteo ferry is about to load up. Walking back to my car, I've been thinking about my mother and not the ferry, remarkably quiet now in its docking. The boathouse is gone, "Losvar" simply a name scrolled in iron and bleeding rust down the walls of Mukilteo's dockside condominiums. The attendant in her orange vest has waved disembarking traffic up the hill and now points at the ferry with her left hand and gestures at Lane 2 with her right. I get in and start my car, straighten out, and drive down the steel ramp and onto the car deck of the *Kittitas*, park in line, lock up, and squeeze my way through the lined-up cars and up the stairs onto the passenger deck to wait.

At eighty-five, my mother is having trouble speaking and arranging her things, the papers and bills piling up around her. This is unlike her, I know, looking out the window at Hat Island some six nautical miles due north. The *Kittitas* has backed out almost imperceptibly from the Mukilteo landing, the big smooth diesels humming through the deck. It's a short ride from Mukilteo to Clinton, but time enough to wonder. Why didn't she teach me how to play the organ? For years I thought she couldn't be bothered, but that wasn't it.

And it has taken a generation skip for me to understand. As I think back, maybe it was as simple as my mother's not being able to read music. My daughter, whose music teacher grew frustrated trying to impress on her the importance of reading music, plays by ear, a trait she inherited from her grandmother. All through my daughter's flute and piano lessons, she played by memory and instinct, and arranged her music stand neatly during eighth-grade band concerts because she was supposed to. Perhaps my mother felt she was supposed to read the notes as well, although I never saw sheet music above her keyboard. "On the Sunny Side of the Street" or "Lazy River," each was her own internal rendition, her own lovely self-indulgence. The real dilemma for my mother, I believe, was that she had always been dutiful and conscientious to a fault about a set of expectations. She was the obedient girl, following the 1950s script of domesticity and authority. The "oughts" and "shoulds." Her measure? Clean floors and dinner on the table, perhaps even perfect children to be seen and not heard. Then I came along.

☉   ☉   ☉

"How did this trombone get dented?" my mother asked the next time she opened the case, which looked like it had been kicked down a flight of stairs.

"I don't know," I said, and I didn't. I could speculate, rubbing the dents at the bottom of the slide and small indentation in the horn. "Maybe the slide fell off." Maybe I shouldn't have thrashed my way through Scotch broom and scrub pine, off the path then on again, to save five extra blocks on the walk home from school. Maybe a trombone case made a poor shield.

"I wish you'd learn some responsibility," she said. "Learn to take care of your things." It was her long-standing wish in terms of my room, my desk at school, my clothes, my life. It still is. There's a way things are supposed to be done from haircuts to shining shoes. Once she even suggested that I could learn a lot about tidiness by joining the army. It was 1967 when she suggested it, sardonically, over drinks one evening with my father, who shook the paper open in front of him to hide his grin. I tried to explain to her that given my luck and the mess in Vietnam, the reward didn't seem worth the risk.

At the end of my sixth-grade year, her solution was to enroll me in summer marching-band camp. Perhaps close-order drill would shape me up. I don't remember learning much during sixth-grade band, but I do remember band camp competing with Little League baseball. As soon as school was out, Little League tryouts were held in Hamlin Park, and every ambitious kid in our neighborhood showed up that Saturday morning. Though my mitt was ragged, one of those hand-me-down amorphous gloves like Enos Slaughter wore during the war, I was confident and skilled at work-up, with a good arm and bat. First base would be fine, but I'd settle for outfield if they were desperate. Four teams held open tryouts and five times as many kids as needed counted off for the split between teams, the Ridgecrest Jaycees getting their chance at me. "Spread out around the infield," someone's father in a red Ridgecrest baseball hat said, pointing from home plate, a ball in his hand and a bat on his shoulder at the ready. "Field the grounder and throw it back to the catcher." Simple enough.

I set myself near second base, mouth open and butterflies in my stomach. A two hopper to me, dust kicking up and through my legs the ball went. I wasn't ready. Around the horn he hit the ball and then another to me, and I knocked it down, picked it out of the dirt, and threw on one hop to the catcher. Wait until he sees me hit, I thought to myself. Then he waved us all to the sidelines and another group of six boys out onto the field.

When this father asked four of us to see him in the dugout, he looked sad and tilted his red Ridgecrest hat back on his head and stuck his hands in his pockets. I looked around at the other three guys, skinny no-talent kids who never scored more than fifty points in a game of five hundred. I heard the man say to them that he was sorry that the team couldn't suit up more players, that there was room for only a few and it was his hard job to tell them that if they worked on their skills they could try out again next year. Then he shook their hands as if closing the deal.

And then he shook mine. I was that slow. I took two hours to walk home through Hamlin Park, trying not to cry. I threw the mitt back into the attic where I'd found it, and cursed my fate, cut in the first round, sad and embarrassed and wronged. My father asked me why I was so upset, and jaw quivering, I told him about the tryout—omitting my arrogance—and blamed my mitt. He said there's always next year and your mother says you have band practice this afternoon.

My lips weren't in it. We practiced in a schoolyard, kicking dust up as we marched in circles behind our drum major, who tried to high-step and blow his whistle at the same time. The trombones, their slides lethal, lined up in the front row and chaos spread out behind us in loose notes and misdirection. I still don't remember the songs. Our two-week camp, day after hazy day of marching and bleating, would culminate with our entry in the Lake City Parade, the Hamlin Park school marching band dressed in their Sunday best and on display. I do remember on that hot asphalt day we marched behind a mounted posse, their rhinestone saddles and shoes clacking. Facing us, Ronnie Smith, our drum major, high-stepped backwards, his scepter aimed at the horses' rears. I yelled at him to stop. He blew his whistle to a beat nobody could follow. Song after song, I moved my slide in time with the girl's next to me because I figured she knew what to play, and marched to my own drummer, avoiding the horse crap in the road. I feared we'd never make it to the end of the parade, stalled or kicked or stampeded or rear-ended by our own tubas. It felt like band camp would never be over.

On several occasion I have tried to explain and even apologize to my mother for my lack of interest in the trombone and band camp. To confess, my mind was elsewhere, for a small success had come my way, a turn, as Frost might say, that "made all the difference." A week after my ignominious release from the Ridgecrest tryouts, Mickey Scott, my nemesis across the street, said I should come to the North City Merchants workout because they needed more players and maybe a spastic like me might get lucky. And I did. I borrowed Bobby Siegfried's glove, an oiled Wilson with a good pocket. Relegated to deep right field, I heard the man in the green cap at home plate say throw to first base and then saw him fungo the ball high and to my left. Back I went, shading my eyes with the glove all the way to the fence, and watched the ball drop soundly into my glove. Then I threw the ball as hard as I could, a frozen rope three feet off the ground all the way home, dust popping off the catcher's mitt.

Shaking his hand, the catcher flipped the ball to the man, who yelled out to me, "I said first base." I thought I had blown this chance too, but they asked me back the next day and again the next, and when they read the final roster a week later, my name was the last one called. I had a position now, and the first of many athletic uniforms in my life. I was on my way. I couldn't have been happier.

✷   ✷   ✷

Caught on a ferryboat between islands, I wonder what happened to my trombone. My mother gave up on my music career and accompanied my father as he followed my playing baseball and then basketball all the way through college. But I'm sure she has never given up on how I am supposed to behave. Sometimes when she played "When You're Smiling," she wasn't smiling, but as the years went by, I blamed myself less and less, given hindsight and a long time to think about what she must have experienced growing up in the 1930s and '40s. I began to understand that she was a young woman caught between her own spontaneity and her sense of duty.

Because she has little room now, she gave me her photo albums for safekeeping and in them she is lovely before the war. In one photo, she's holding old-fashioned wooden skis, her jacket off, squinting for the snow-bright day at White Pass. Although the photos are black and white, I know her eyes are hazel, a word I have loved for years. In another, my father and she are dancing, smiling beside a table with drinks and ashtrays. In another, my father sits behind her on the Hat Island cabin steps, her head resting back on his chest, his right hand holding her forehead as if she has a fever though she's smiling with her eyes closed. In another, they both stand next to the new DeSoto my father had won in 1941 in a fishing derby in Seattle, their first car, which they sold a year later when my father went off to war.

When he came back in 1945, I imagine things were different, as they were for many young couples—great relief followed by great domestic realignment. I was born nine months later. My mother and father had very little besides each other, his willingness to work and her sense of duty to the neighbors, to propriety, to what the world thought, to dinner on the table, to cleanliness and shined shoes. My mother had liked working during the war, but afterward vacillated between working and staying home, often turning down promotions, then quitting to keep house. All through my growing up, I remember her leaving in the morning for some job—the bank, the credit agency, the utility department, the property management office. Then, as if two kids and the stops on her organ called her back to a domestic life, she found herself, ironically, trapped at home again.

Often when I was home from college during a break, I would wake late at night to find my mother sitting in her kitchen smoking her Kent cigarettes and looking out the window. "I need to get out of here," she said once, and I was too surprised by her cryptic remark to ask why. Out of this house? Her life? Her obligations? I just nodded, feeling closer to her. "Why didn't my mother make a fuss over me? I asked her that once, you know."

"Did she have an answer?" I asked.

"She was surprised. 'We just thought you knew what you were doing,' was all she said."

I realized then that my mother had been dutiful and self-sufficient and proper for a long time, worried that others might think ill of her or that they might not think of her at all. Growing up, I had no way of knowing why my mother looked pensive or how anger is a natural response to fear. It was the early '50s outside the city limits of Seattle, with no two houses the same distance from their common gravel road, and many mothers in our neighborhood seemed anxious. My mother collected dimes for the children in iron lungs. I remember the worried look on her face when I told her how we crawled under our desks at school and practiced "duck and cover" in case the Russians dropped the bomb. I remember the red lights sweeping our windows one night when the ambulance came to pick up Ruth Scott across the street and take her to the Hamlin Park TB Sanitarium. I feared the semiannual visit to the doctor—its booster shots and tests—and I remember after one of those visits the breath my mother took in when she pulled the Band-Aid off my skinny back because it itched so. Then we were back in the pediatrician's office and he pushed a tiny needle beneath the skin of my nine-year-old arm. Two days later the welt rose up worse than a bee sting. It was 1955. My TB test was positive. I had no idea what that meant besides my mother looking grim enough to cry.

Maybe she thought it was her fault, though I'm sure she knew it wasn't. She made me rest, even though the doctor explained that the X ray showed that the few TB spots I had on my lung had calcified. And despite her admonitions for me to stay on our side of the street, I walked with Mickey Scott one day to see his mother at Hamlin Park. We stood beside the sanitarium building, and three stories up, Ruth Scott leaned out the window, her mouth covered with Kleenex to protect us. She said she was sorry, so sorry. I didn't know what she meant. Sorry for what? And several weeks later Mickey Scott gave me a stuffed toy dog his mother had made for me out of curtain remnants and furniture upholstery. My mother has since told me that she never blamed Ruth Scott for my positive TB test. But they were not friends again. I remember my mother washing the toy dog and hanging it on the line to dry in the silent noonday sun. "What more could I have done?" my mother has wondered out loud.

◌　◌　◌

The ferry is turning toward the Clinton dock and the loudspeaker calls us down to our cars. What have I got to say for myself this time? I'll have a story when I arrive and an argument. I'm curious as always at her response. On one trip back home a few years ago, for example, my mother said to me in front of friends and neighbors, "Read us one of your poems." I had been teaching literature and had published a book of poems; school was out for the summer, and my wife and I were visiting my parents in Tacoma to celebrate my birthday, the Fourth of July. As he did every Fourth of July, my father barbecued salmon he'd caught on one of his trips to Westport, and my mother made potato salad and green salad and baked beans and set the picnic table on their backyard patio. The neighbors were there to say hello. My father had fixed everyone a drink and turned his salmon fillets as I opened my book and read a poem which, I felt, celebrated a boy's unwitting and unwilling entry into music and honored that event in memory. I wanted to let my mother know I hadn't forgotten.

After Listening to Jack Teagarden

I will blame him,
the man who convinced my mother
there was talent in long arms,
whose baton held me lock-stepped
all summer in three songs,
who never revealed the old name
for trombone is sackbut,
as awkward as the black vinyl case
I banged against my knees
in a neighborhood where salvation
meant running. *Sackbut,*
the first girl I ever kissed,
wet-mouthed and blowing
and not a sound, much less a sob
of music. I blame him
for one lost summer, my mouth full of oil,
stuck spit valves, the slide
dented over and over again by the ground.
Yes, him, for my bird-flushing,
window-rattling squawks,

for the anonymous gift of a mute,
for my memory of him yet
like the music stand I could never fold
right again. May he hear me
once more in the Lake City Parade,
timed by his whistle,
all oxfords and a new white shirt.
May he forgive my faking
the two songs I never learned.
May he accept the blame
for my marching out of step up the rear
of the Ridgecrest Mounted Posse,
their horses farting
as I lost myself in "Sweet Georgia Brown,"
the only song I remembered,
as loud as I could.

My father, who was hard of hearing, held up his spatula and smiled. My mother and her neighbor Mrs. Bowers looked at each other. I thought I should explain how I'd designed my poem after a William Stafford poem in which he used the word "accuse" as a refrain, and how I admired Elizabeth Bishop's poem "Filling Station," in which the speaker observes detail after homey service station detail until her cynicism transforms into "somebody loves us all."

But my mother spoke first, "You got that published?"

One more statement submarined by a question. I was still Rootie Kazootie, cymbals tied to my knees, back from the woods on her doorstep, washboard in hand, and speechless. I started to explain, but my mother set her drink on the picnic table and said she'd be right back.

"I thought it was nice that you could remember so much," Mrs. Bowers said. My wife, Penny, busied herself with the table and tried not to laugh. My father turned and basted his salmon fillets. I talked on about having to alter a few details for the sake of the poem, how I grew to appreciate jazz trombonists like Tommy Dorsey and Jack Teagarden, and then my mother returned and handed me a photograph I'd never seen before.

On the sidewalk along the route of the Lake City Parade she has waited in the sun to take this black-and-white photo of me marching with the Hamlin Park summer camp band. I am wearing a white shirt, salt-and-pepper cords, and oxfords that cut into the high instep of my feet. I am in the front row. My cowlick sticks out despite the Vitalis. I see that I'm out of step, given the girl next to me, but I'm blowing into that horn, eyes focused on the slide and cheeks bulging.

"That's for you," my mother said, smiling now.

"I never saw you," I said.

"No, you didn't," she said, and lifted her weeping glass to toast my words, better late than never.

Let Me Be Richard

Let me fix my grandmother's brooch, the one I rifled, a stone pried loose and hidden. I was ten. Might I reset its light? Did I think she wouldn't see the empty place? Had my grandmother blamed the stone's loss on careless packing when she moved from her Greenwood home in Seattle to a back room let by women who forbade her, newly divorced, from sitting in their living room? On Wednesdays, my mother and I would take the bus downtown to see my grandmother in the shoe department on the basement floor of the Bon Marché, where she rang up oxfords and pumps two days a week—her receipts and cash sucked into tubes leading straight to heaven. On weekends, we visited her in a stranger's kitchen, the tea and cookies from one allotted cupboard, an extra chair borrowed for my mother. I leaned against a counter, my feet slipping on the floor's black-and-white tile, and fiddled with the mismatched napkins beside a shiny toaster that magnified half my embarrassed face. In the early 1950s, a rented room was what my grandmother could afford.

What was I thinking, hiding that stolen rhinestone and two crow feathers beneath our backyard willow? Shy and lost at ten, perhaps I wanted a dazzling secret, buried and protected, something for which only I knew the whereabouts. Perhaps I merely wanted to avoid my mother, who had not seen me cover the glass stone with soil, tiny in the mind now and one fewer thing, I concluded, for her to be cross about.

Fifty-five years later, I remember my grandmother as a slight woman stooped as a willow, descending into my parents' kitchen from her room above the garage, a single bed made, a bedside table where she kept a two-dollar bill, its corner torn off so the bad luck would pour out, and three silver dollars, each minted in 1921, three years after the death of her second son. Beside her prayer book, a box of Kleenex that smelled like lilacs. Just now over the fence, lilacs steal into our backyard in Iowa City, the neighbor having not pruned them in the twenty-six years we have lived here. I don't mind. My grandmother blooms each spring and fills the yard with her silent air, her faded print dress, sweater sleeves pushed up, her elbows dabbed with ointment and Saran wrapped for the psoriasis, her white hair permed and combed and held by a clasp.

Let me sit her now at my parents' kitchen table in 1967, my third year away at college, Grandmother's arms crossed to hold an elbow in each hand. She asks my father—as she did every morning for six years—if she may have a cup of coffee. It drives him crazy. His jaw tightens. He pushes his own cup, handle away, toward the center of the kitchen table. Her asking like this tears at the very fabric of our house. It is more threatening to my parents' marriage than her falling the last two cement steps onto the patio while my father barbecued salmon and my mother set the picnic table with silverware and dishes and the potato salad my grandmother had spent the morning fixing.

She fell on my birthday, the Fourth of July. Every year my card from her held three dollars—the price of a rhinestone brooch? But on this one Fourth the ambulance trumped all, a broken hip and wrist the diagnosis, eyeglasses shattered and her left eye blackened. *That's not the problem in this house*, my father said, though he was upset. Neither was it all the burners on the stove left on high, the back wall scorched, nor the days the sink overflowed. Nor the broken glass on the floor, nor my grandmother wandering down the street in her nightgown during a spring rain. *If the woman would just make herself at home*, my father said. That's what drove him crazy. Asking for a cup of coffee.

Maybe my grandmother mistrusted the idea of home—or simply knew home as a stage for loss—ever since she opened her front door in 1918 as her infant boy turned blue on her bed. Outside she found the street empty, the neighbors indoors wearing gauze masks and pulling the curtains back to watch the woman next door ask the sky for help, the flu everywhere. Now I trace the baby's name and the dates my grandmother wrote in pencil on the back page of *Wedding Blossoms*, her thin keepsake book, given to my mother who gave it to me—Donald born September 30, 1917, died December 2, 1918. He was my grandmother's second of four children: Marion the youngest, and before her my mother, and my uncle Richard, the oldest. My grandmother wrote their names in fountain-pen longhand, as if to make their lives indelible. Marion the baby and beautiful. My mother, Lois, in the middle, dutiful. Richard at the top, the favorite.

My mother also gave me her own photo albums and the few family documents she could find, so I might better remember her mother. In photo after photo my grandmother looks directly at the camera, looking away only in the few taken with Richard. In those she gazes at him: Richard, the son who left home early to join the merchant marine corps. Maybe he needed to escape his father, my grandfather, a large, sleeve-gartered, surly man who smoked Chesterfields and loved to eat. For this German from Vermont, my grandmother changed her name from

McCullough to Hahneman. McCullough was the surname on her birth certificate, issued in 1948 by John Edgar, clerk of the Orphan's Court of the Commonwealth of Pennsylvania. My grandmother was born in 1895, but this birth certificate was entered into the delayed birth record docket fifty-three years later. Why? For welfare's sake? For work? And what is an orphan's court? I don't know. Proof of the rumor in the family that my grandmother was adopted— her first abandonment?

Her first name was Mary, her middle name Alma, someone nourishing and kind and a whisper of a soul by the time I knew her. In the end, her married name provided no home at all, for my grandfather left to search Alaska for work and a better mood. Then, once back home, he left my grandmother for Hazel, the woman in the apartment upstairs, the woman who made gingerbread and played canasta. My mother's eyes blazed at every mention of her name.

What is there to remember besides the breeze lifting the lace curtains in my grandmother's silent back room, the dominoes laid end to end on the table, my mother tidying, my grandmother folded into a chair, her hands crippled by arthritis, aggravated some say by feeling resentful and unloved? Was there joy? Laughter? Of course. There was always Richard, who lived in Walnut Creek, California, and loved good food. Richard, who had sailed the seas as a young man, visiting China and Japan, stood five inches taller than his two sisters, arms around each in the photo my father took in 1956. My uncle Richard barked at his wife, Nellie, who barked right back, cigarette ash flying. Tidy and fastidious, he organized by color and purpose every piece of his clothing. He arranged his triangles by size and his pencils by length, so he could draw the nuts and bolts of steel bridges. Although he suffered the same diabetes as his father, Uncle Richard poured himself four martinis every night, and when his mother was visiting, limited her to three.

She could stay as long as she wished, he insisted, my grandmother who smoked only in Walnut Creek—though she held the cigarette over her head and never inhaled—who loved trips to Reno, my uncle and aunt and grandmother driving up to stay the night and play the nickel slot machines all evening. If my grandmother hit a jackpot, lights flashing, she'd grin and wave at Richard, who scooped the nickels and moved her to a new machine. An hour later, my grandmother's hands black from the coins, her cardboard coin bucket empty, she'd call again. "Not long now," Richard would say and fill the bucket and stand behind her to watch, pull after enthusiastic pull. My uncle Richard: dark haired, long in the waist, a narrow face and a wide smile. I look like him. My grandmother would play the piano for him in Walnut Creek, numbers like "Make Believe" or "How About Me?" or maybe a chorus of two-step ragtime she had learned as a girl, hired for a dollar to play in theaters, a voice for the silent movies.

Then Richard was silent, a heart attack one morning as he reached for the newspaper on his sidewalk. He was forty-nine.

My father answered the telephone on Christmas Eve 1965. Sitting beside our decorated tree, my grandmother, back a month from her visit to California, her son's yearly gift of See's chocolates in her lap, didn't make a sound. What song do you play for such a loss? After Richard died, she slipped away year by year into dementia, hardening of the arteries, my mother said. When my father gave his ultimatum—*Her or me*—my mother moved her mother into a nursing home. We packed her clothes (fragrance of lilacs and tissue up her sleeve) and her silver dollars, her new glasses, and Grandma's little book of photos. Home from teaching across the state, I had much to tell my grandmother about my new job, but my parents' house that day felt like a funeral home. Only whispers would do. Trying to be helpful, I carried her suitcase downstairs and out to the car. She carried her thoughts on a string of sentence fragments that spilled what she was thinking. She was cold, I remember, and wore every sweater she had.

⊘　⊘　⊘

On my visits to her in the nursing home, she would offer to make toasted cheese sandwiches with tomato soup, although she had no kitchen. She would walk me down the hall and introduce me to her neighbor, a woman whose name she couldn't remember. "Hello," my grandmother would say, "This is my son, Richard."

"No, Grandma, I'm your grandson, Jim," I'd say, maybe a little hurt that she had forgotten me. But what did I know?

"Oh, yes," she'd say until my next visit or even later that day, when she would brighten suddenly and introduce me again, "This is my son, Richard." Finally I thought, let me be Richard. I stole something from her a long time ago, and now at least I can pry my own name loose and return her son, bowing as he might have done after each of her nickel jackpots.

One day my mother called. "Your grandmother has pneumonia," she said, the old person's friend. "Do you want to see her?" I said yes. But when I arrived, my grandmother was unaware of me. She lay gasping, the blanket up to her chin, the satin edge rolled between her thumb and forefinger, a child's first caress and the last to leave. The lilacs are blooming next door. I remember my grandmother's arms were scarred, a boiling pot spilled when she was young. Against all reason, her scars grew younger every year. Let me turn the handles back into the stove.

When the young doctor asked my mother if he should take any measures, my mother—so unused to doing nothing even when there's nothing left to do—said no. Then there was only Richard left, the man I look like in my silence.

Payoff

Signing another house payment check, I think of my mother in 1984 when she announced they had saved enough to pay off the mortgage on their three-bedroom rambler, purchased twenty-six years earlier. Home for a visit, I asked her what interest rate she was paying, if that wasn't too nosy. Three percent, she said. "But Mom," I said, "don't pay it off. You could make a little by just putting the lump sum in the bank." My father and mother bought the house in 1958 for sixteen thousand dollars. They watched it being built by Mr. Wick, the contractor who built one design eight different ways up and down Huson Drive in Tacoma, Washington. The house had shingle siding, oak floors, composition roof, a fireplace, fir trees in the backyard, and a view of Mount Rainier. It was my parents' first and only new house.

"Oh, I don't want the trouble of writing checks anymore," she said. I tried to explain that she could have payments automatically deducted, that the current interest was eight percent, which meant she could make five percent on her money by doing nothing. It made good business sense to me. "Well, that sounds like a possibility. Let me ask your father," she said.

I had a good idea what she would do. It was Saturday, her canning day, and I talked on about credit and rates as she arranged mason jars on the counter and asked me to lift down the fifteen-quart pressure cooker from the cupboard in the utility room, iron and first-generation, and set it in the sink so she might rinse it out. I can't remember whether my father had been salmon fishing again or she had discovered another bumper crop of green beans, a bushel to stock her pantry, the idea of enough always just around the corner. Canning was her bank against the future—mason jars, washed salmon fillets, oil, salt, the lids and rim locks.

My mother died at eighty-eight in 2008, the lid on for good. My father had been dead for fifteen years. She never mentioned her mortgage again, just as she never let on about what business or concerns boiled up between my father and her all those years of my brother's and my living at home, dinner always ready, the holidays festooned, a fire in the fireplace, backyards and ballgames, long languorous summer evenings. A Beaver Cleaver existence, my brother says. The warm twilight sleep of childhood. How did they pull that off for us? What weren't they telling us? What did they hold back? I never asked such questions then, being far too "green and carefree" as the Welsh poet says.

When my mother grew more and more infirm, my brother and his wife looked after her. My wife and I volunteered, said come live with us in Iowa, we'll take care of you. But, no. She understood my brother. For years, my mother and father could only guess what I was up to, and as ambitious and encouraging as they were for my wandering, my mother felt safer with the familiar. In her last apartment, my brother lifted her from her wheelchair to the bed, cleaned her, and washed her soiled clothing. He was her favorite child, my aunt always said. I was firstborn and first out the door. He was second and stayed at home, whining and moping on the couch. She would fuss, cleaning up after him when he threw up at age six, helpless at the prospect of going four blocks down the hill to school. At the end of her life she was helpless and my brother understood that.

Thinking back, I realize how much I took my parents and their house for granted, how much I ran my heedless ways and returned unannounced. But then again, my father and mother made it easy to do that, a meal ready from the earliest I remember, rumpled and dusty, to whenever my wife and I stopped by with their granddaughter. My father would take our coats, mix drinks, my mother puttering in the kitchen, the talk over dinner easy, about food or friends or trips they were about to take. "It's comfortable here," my wife said, who had grown up in a house where the "chronic angers" seemed far more palpable. In my most suspicious moments, I think my parents withheld the uncomfortable details about themselves, especially in regard to their history. My family's great, varnished silence.

I'm sure my parents suffered their own angers. Both of them grew up during the 1920s and '30s. Both came from broken households. When his mother and father split in the early '30s, my father left to ride the rails to eastern Washington to harvest wheat. He was seventeen. Finishing high school was out of the question. My father and mother married in 1941, but soon thereafter my father joined the Seabees and my mother found work with the government to supplement her family's ration coupons. She scrimped and saved. My brother told me that despite our mother's wishes, our father wouldn't consider kids before he left for the war, that he didn't want his new wife at home pregnant and him dead on the beaches of Guam or Okinawa. Left on her own, she worked the two and a half years my father was away. He survived, despite the war's unimaginable horrors.

But where was the tension in their voices? The narrative dislocation? The emotional complication? I remember her voice steady behind their closed bedroom door or whispered into the telephone when my father traveled to Idaho and Montana on business. Those nights, she would sit up late at her kitchen table, smoking and shuffling a stack of bills before her. Whatever troubles my parents may have had, they kept the lid on. Home, my father seemed comfortable in his easy chair or in the backyard tending his flower garden, but I suspect my mother felt frustrated for a long time, telling my brother once that she regretted giving up her government job when my dad returned from the war. She had babies and kept house. Tired of that, she found work and felt both guilty and angry, I imagine, torn between raising her kids and making ends meet. Once when I was home from college, for example, rummaging in the cupboard above her washer and dryer looking for soap to wash my clothes—Tide, of course, and All, to symbolize her eternal scouring—I found white cloth sacks full of flour squatting like fat government officials, stencil marked "U.S. Surplus: Not to be Sold." Were my folks on welfare? I re-hid the sacks.

And never asked. She never spoke of them. I never saw the sacks again, though I mentioned them to my brother, who said money had always been an issue. Evidence to the contrary, what I remember is plenty. Home was the wicker cornucopia my mother dragged out on holidays and filled with apples and walnuts and almonds for the table centerpiece. If the night held disappointment, morning waited for me with Frosted Flakes, a prize inside every box, with a spoonful of sugar added to each bowl and then milk. Sugar, that postwar luxury she could now afford. Of course, having no idea what it meant to ration anything, I wanted to eat my way to the prize in one sitting. Wait, my mother said. Lunch was always in a hurry—bologna or tuna fish sandwiches wrapped in wax paper, with an apple or carrots or a pickle that dripped on the table at school. Depression meals, my wife has said. I didn't notice, baseball calling or my bike ready to ride or the bus pulling up to its stop.

Maybe the aura of plenty is what they gathered around them, especially in their neighbors and friends. Much of what I remember has to do with their gathering and preparing and serving food. After my mother died, my brother gave me a cardboard box of her loose photographs, where I found myself as a two-year-old beer swiller at Hat Island. World War II had been over for three years. Snapshot after snapshot shows communal feasts being prepared by those who spent their summers in cabins lining the beach on Puget Sound. Hat Island is six nautical miles from Mukilteo and Everett, Washington. During the 1930s through the '40s and '50s, people hand-crafted cabins from scavenged lumber and driftwood, using cedar logs for shakes and creosote-soaked planks for boardwalks; they anchored buoys off the beach for the outboard boats that were the only access to the island. No electricity, foul outhouses, iceboxes with foot-square ice blocks hauled over in burlap from the mainland, water from the catch barrels beneath clay banks on the far side of the bay.

One photo shows my father in overalls and a baseball hat standing between John Carlson, my dad's best friend, and Bunny Carlson, John's nephew, who's bareheaded and wearing a rain slicker. Each holds two king salmon that must weigh fifteen pounds apiece. Before them on a board on the sand lie eighteen more salmon, kings and cohos five pounds to twenty-five pounds each. There must be over two hundred pounds of fish in this photograph, and this after one day's fishing. "Didn't they have limits in 1948?" I asked my dad once and he said yes, of course they did, and winked to confirm his choice between the government and feeding his neighbors.

John's wife, Helen, who always carried a Brownie camera, must have taken this picture. As if the Sound had blessed them, as if their lives had been spared, each man is smiling. As if finally there was enough to go around. As

if the time had come when men, now home from a hos-
tile world, could sit down with their wives and children,
as if the past had been settled, a tide ebbed, the kicker
boats run up on shore, their island secure and bountiful.
In another photograph, my dad looks at the camera while
Bunny and John look at the fish they are holding, amazed
at their luck. Up by the cabin, a table is being set. The
photo shows planks laid out on sawhorses, the table so
big it takes two tablecloths to cover it. The seat on each
side of the table is a plank set on a bench on one end and
a chair on the other. My mother stands to one side and
smokes. In a bathing cap and wrapped in a towel, Mrs.
Pacini memorializes her swim in the Sound. In the next
photo the table has been set with fifteen places. Bowls and
dishes of salad and vegetables, and bread and fruit grace
the middle. My mother sits on one bench with her back
to the table comforting me in her lap for all my fussing, I
imagine, or whining. All are seated in another photo, the
Carlsons, the Dukes, the Pacinis, and the McKeans, my
dad still in his overalls and baseball hat passing the bread.
It's a sunny day. The adults wear hats and speak side to
side and fill their plates. It might explain why, in the last
photograph, John Carlson, "Swede," my father called him,
bald, suspendered, work shirt and scuffed boots, union
man and card-holding communist, who shared up and
down the island's boardwalk his weekly English *Pravda*,
sits back against the side of his cabin and smiles around
his pipe after the meal shared by everyone.

⊘   ⊘   ⊘

Gathering was my parents' ongoing occupation. Did they
practice subsistence living? I wonder and then worry
about the definition—need it mean poor? Subsistence as
a minimum for survival, the least needed to stay alive?

Were those the stakes behind my father's obsession? Every chance he got, my father fished north at Sekiu on the Olympic Peninsula and south at Westport and Ilwaco on the mouth of the Columbia River. Later in his life he picked blackberries, wandering the neighborhood backyards and empty lots and coming home scratched and dusty to pour his blackberries into a sieve in the kitchen sink. He expected pie and my mother obliged, processing food in the kitchen her great weekend industry. After mornings picking cucumbers, peaches, strawberries, cherries, beans, or after a fishing trip when my father took his largest king salmon and had it kippered in the smokehouse in Westport, the fillets scored and coated with sugar and cook-smoked and wrapped in oil paper, then the good work began. When my father carried the full boxes through the back door, the redolence of smoked salmon filled the kitchen. My mother washed her stock of mason jars. My father found the pressure cooker and set it in the sink. I would fiddle with its relief valve and tap the glass on the pressure gauge. They parceled out new lids and washed them. They measured out salmon or beans or pickles and packed the jars and fitted them with new flat lids and sealed them down with the ring locks. Ten jars lined the pressure cooker, which my father filled with the appropriate level of water, tightened the lid with the six plastic screw downs, and lifted the heavy cooker onto the burner.

Although they knew the pressure figures and the approximate time needed to seal the jars, my mother and father waited in the kitchen, my mother smoking or cleaning up or making lunch for my father and me. Each step elaborated the ritual, from the cleaned fresh salmon lying in the backyard for pictures to the sealed mason jars lining the shelves in our garage, in the utility room, even the shelves of our bedrooms. But I wasn't thinking as much then as I was immersed in the smells and sounds of the kitchen. It had never been any different.

And my mother and father, who never spoke much during this work, seemed to know by rote the steps in this process and never said what each step meant to them as the stove heated and the pressure cooker ticked and swelled. But now I wonder if this first-generation cast-iron pressure cooker suggests more about my parents' relationship than they would ever have thought or chosen to explain. Famous for its "jiggle top," the weighted pressure regulator that sits atop a vent pipe, the cooker heats up until steam spits and hisses through the regulator, which starts to rock and agitate. Then you lower the heat until the regulator is moving only three to five times a minute, the pressure constant and the steam a soft hissing, until it's time to shut the heat down. Yes, that seems like them. And when my father lifted the cooker off the stove and set it in the sink and ran water across its sides to cool it—called a "cold water release"—we all waited and finally, beneath that bolted lid, a "ping" sounded and then another until all ten mason jars had sealed themselves.

That "ping" meant my mother and father had sealed their lives against want, that they could feed my brother and me and themselves and be sure of that. Growing up, despite the Movietone Korean War, the polio and tuberculosis in our neighborhood, despite the "duck and cover" drills at school, and *The War of the Worlds* at the Ridgecrest Theater on Saturday, I never thought the future was in doubt. Angry or frightened maybe, my mother would wringer-wash more clothes, the smell of Clorox throughout the house. Every opportunity he had, my father would fish, a sane way for him to spend his time and feed his family as well.

Money was useful and when he and my mother had a little saved up, he asked her out of curiosity and perhaps amusement, "What are we going to do with it all?" My mother was far more provident. She grew up in the Depression as well, "when there never seemed to be enough to go around," she said on occasion. Prone to the morose, her father spent long hours at work or months at a time in Alaska. Her mother waited in silence. Her sister and brother wandered off into their own lives. In retrospect I'm sure my mother, haunted by ambivalence, had serious doubts about the choices she made, ambitious on one hand and a good girl on the other, self-effacing and dutiful and silent enough to resent it.

But what did I know, growing up around my parents? I knew that fresh coho and king salmon were ours after a morning's fishing, that Dungeness crab filled the traps across Hat Island's bay, that butter clams spilled from our shovels at low tide and would spit their sand out all day when we hung them in burlap bags from the buoys. I knew that roasted salmon, cracked crab, and steamed clams went best with drawn butter and chopped shallots, though I couldn't explain that then, being young and hungry and sure the whole world ate this way. It is still delicious even in memory. Was this how they tightened their belts? Kept the wolf from the door and their heads above water? Perhaps. Subsistence? Other definitions suggest subsistence is a real and meaningful existence, an essence, an underlying reality. Salmon as essence, I think now, what they caught or trapped or dug the bounty to be celebrated in the moment. A feast to keep the body and soul together.

I can tell you now that despite my well-intentioned argument, my mother paid the full amount of her mortgage four years before it was due. She never explained. Convenience? Opportunity? I don't think so. Was she uncomfortable with the bank dipping into her account every month? Well, there may have been something to that, but doing nothing was not an option. I can't help but think my mother's signing that check, licking the envelope, the stamp, writing out her return address and the bank's name and address in her good Palmer script, and then walking the letter out to the postbox, served as a kind of financial "ping" that eliminated the vagaries and spoilage of credit. Circumstance, the times, a family breakup, and poverty had taken much from her, but she had survived and now owned her home, furnished and cupboards full. Like so many in her generation, she was a reasonable credit risk, reliable as yesterday and good for tomorrow, self-sustaining, no longer poor, standing arms akimbo next to her mailbox, the flag raised as if to claim this house as "mine."

Queen for a Day

Setting down a box marked "Grandma Hattie" on the floor of our living room, my wife, Penny, explains that it was sad when her parents left her at her grandma's house, but she was always glad to see her grandma. "Her house was special." Penny remembers climbing the stairs into her grandmother's attic, lifting the heavy trunk lid to the embrace of cedar and mothballs, and looking in. It was the first permission she asked for after being dropped off each Friday afternoon.

Grandma Hattie's cats followed her from the attic to the kitchen to the swing in the backyard, built by her grandfather. She remembers the light above the sink and cleaning vegetables from the garden and grace before every meal. Always cake or pie after dinner and an hour of TV, maybe Lawrence Welk on the black-and-white TV set, the rabbit ears adjusted to stop the screen from rolling. After "Adios, Au Revoir, Auf Wiedersehen," Grandpa George, who smoked cigars and snored, made his way to his own bedroom. Six or seven at the time, Penny found her pajamas, washed her face, brushed her teeth, and climbed up into the big bed next to Grandma Hattie, her Raggedy Ann, newly clothed in old remnants, tucked in beneath the flannel and down and the warm cotton sheets.

When I lift the lid of this file box in front of me, the grit of dust and old newsprint settles on my hands. As new grandparents ourselves, Penny and I have our own boxes to sort through. It's an endless task and sometimes difficult deciding what to save and what to shred. I knew Penny's grandmother Hattie for just a few years, the last of her life. As we sort through her box, Penny isn't sure what to do with her grandma's letters and files, newspaper clippings and photos of those long dead. I'm not sure either, until Penny touches my shoulder and reminds me that Grandma Hattie gave our marriage her blessing. Lifting a photo of her grandparents clipped from a newspaper, Penny runs a finger across the yellowing fragment, as if to brush her grandmother's hair back. Well then, if she gave her blessing, all the more reason to see how we might return the favor.

◌   ◌   ◌

The 1958 picture in the *Tri-City Herald,* captioned "Winner," features Mr. and Mrs. G. J. Spangberg, who are seated on their couch reading the letter from Boyd's coffee that congratulates them on picking one of the winning names for the Boyd's mascot "Boidie." Unfortunately, the citation makes no mention of the name she sent in. Grandpa George is seventy-five. Bald, thick in the jowls, he wears a white shirt and tie. He peers down at the letter through wire-rimmed bifocals with a semi-bemused look, his grin not quite reaching the corners of his mouth. It's the same expression he gives straight on looking at you from his obit picture six years later. Penny's Grandma Hattie looks like I've always remembered her. Norwegian with high cheekbones, she has a heart-shaped face. She smiles above her dimpled chin—a feature I see reproduced in my wife and my daughter. Hattie's hair, half-tone gray in the black-and-white photo, is permed in tight curls and swept back off her forehead. Her glasses are lined on the upper lenses with rhinestones and she wears butterfly earrings, a formal dress with a wide, flared collar, and a necklace that sparkles.

This picture was taken years before my introduction to Hattie. I met her at my first Sunday dinner at Penny's parents' house, when Penny and I were dating. Hattie was seated next to me at the table, and Penny was on my right. Before dinner, Penny introduced me. I can't remember what Hattie said to me, but she smiled and took my hand, and then we all sat down.

I began dating Penny in 1973, a year of parades before her parents and relatives, the great aunts from North Dakota and the cousins twice-removed from Astoria, Oregon. I was Penny's "young man," the person of interest, a hand extended and coffee offered. Let's sit and talk, they would say casually, interested in who I was and what I had to say. But an audience with Grandma Hattie carried formal weight and measure.

The year Penny was born was the year Hattie and George Spangberg moved from Pasadena to the Tri-Cities, Washington. Grandma Hattie spoke Norwegian at home when George was alive. But when I first met her, she lived alone and spoke Norwegian only to his memory.

At that dinner with Penny's family, the dishes, the silverware, the cloth napkins that matched the tablecloth, all waited for me like a landscape of hazards. I was not alone in feeling the tension at the table. Penny's father sat at the head, with Penny's grandmother to his right, always the seat for the guest of honor. Hattie lifted her soup spoon and then carefully placed it back down on the table. Her father asked Penny to say grace, and then we all began. Across the table, my future sister-in-law spoke at length about the rain in Seattle and lawn chairs. Robert, her husband, the ex-Navy ensign now real estate broker, was seated on his father-in-law's left. Laughing, these two appeared to know something no one else knew. The glances Grandma

Hattie gave me throughout the dinner flashed like a warning. Uncertain about what to say, I spoke of basketball and my teaching at the local community college. As I reached for the salt, Penny's father said, "Watch your sleeve. The candles should be moved," a comment that made Penny's mother crumple her napkin. When he said, "The potatoes are too dry," Penny's mother pushed her chair back quickly, reached for the bowl and took it to the kitchen. Now the rest of the table clutched at their napkins. Penny's sister nattered on about Seattle. Robert hung on Mr. Lee's every word like an employee, and the food circled counter-clockwise, with Hattie finally nodding at me while passing the peas.

For the most part, Hattie remained silent that evening, moving from the table to the living room after dinner, keeping her own counsel. Then after some imperceptible signal to her son-in-law, she was helped into her coat and escorted to the door and driven home by Mr. Lee. Penny told me then that her grandma had been living alone in her house for the last nine years, her second husband, George, having died in 1964. Although mention had been made about moving her to more comfortable and supervised quarters, Hattie did not want to leave her house and her garden.

◇   ◇   ◇

George and Hattie Spangberg moved from Pasadena to Kennewick in 1953. A photo in a 1956 edition of the *Tri-City Herald* features the couple standing on their front porch, proud of the house they have spent three years renovating. The heading for the companion article reads, "'Plain' Ranch House Converted Into Real 'Home of Distinction.'" On the same page, there's a column titled "The Way I See It," written by her son-in-law, the publisher of the *Tri-City Herald*, arguing vehemently against trade unions.

I've always wondered why Hattie, maybe seventy years old and married for a second time to a retired butcher named George, would sell their comfortable bungalow in Pasadena, a retirement paradise at the time, and move to the desert of southeastern Washington State. Why buy a modest ranch house in the tiny, dusty community of Kennewick? In the photo George wears a plaid shirt, but Hattie looks ready in her day dress and fresh perm for a gathering of the church auxiliary. Penny remembers the church women who thought the world of Hattie Spangberg. She stood for kindness and hard work in the Lutheran community, the last one to leave after the church supper, cleaning up and wiping down. Her cherry pies and cakes and cookies at Christmas graced the pastor's plate. Maybe this is what grandmothers were supposed to do when Penny was growing up, what Christian women were supposed to do.

But why did Hattie move? I think her son-in-law, Glenn, asked her to join them in the Tri-Cities. It was August of 1953. According to Senator McCarthy, there were communists everywhere. The Russians had just exploded their first hydrogen bomb, the Rosenbergs had been executed, and now there was a new baby, Glenn Lee's fourth child and third daughter, born twelve years after her closest sibling, her mother over forty and still bound, by choice or obligation, to the social commitments expected of the wife of the local newspaper publisher, one who was fighting a newspaper war. Glenn suspected the International Typesetters Union had been secretly funding a rival newspaper, the *Columbia Basin News*, while striking his own paper, the pickets on duty every day. The pressure was immense. Penny's older siblings, teenagers now, were trying to survive pressures at school. His wife sought solace with her friends at the country club. The telephone at home rang late in the night with threats or worse, silence at the other end of the line. Years later in a box of Glenn Lee's papers, Penny and I found the .38 revolver he carried to work.

Penny also found a letter he saved, which begins, "Dear Glenn: We received your paper and were surprised to see the strike was still on. What is the matter with the newspaper assoc.? Can't they step in and help? Newspapers should stick together in a case like this, I should think—help one another. My land, this has been going on a long time. How long are you going to be able to hang on?"

Part of the letter is given over to a list of scriptural references Hattie titled, "I WILL HELP THEE." In the body she relates news about the weather in Pasadena, how they have settled in after a vacation, how her friends have been holding up over the winter. She asks about the asparagus crops in eastern Washington and how Myrt (Glenn's sister) is doing and then signs off by saying, "Lots of love to Elaine and yourself, and don't forget the little punks." The letter is typed and she writes "Mom & Pop" in red pencil. Then she must have wound the letter back into the typewriter and written "Last night I was a Mother at a Mother and Daughter Banquet at the church. Mrs. Geo. Hendrickson asked me to be her Mother. Lovely program. Tonight Pop gives a travel talk at the Sons of Norway." And then she signs again in red pencil, "Mom & Pop."

Penny's father saved this letter in a business envelope along with several clippings Grandma Hattie must have included: "How to Conquer Your Fears" by Norman Vincent Peale, and a tract from the Norwegian Lutheran Mission, "Why Worry?" by G. M. Trygstad. I'm not sure Glenn Lee was afraid of much, but I'm guessing he was worried enough about his new baby daughter to convince his mother-in-law to pick up stakes and move, a devoutly Christian woman, a woman born in the nineteenth century, who loved the sphere of her kitchen and garden, the role of housewife and church matron, a woman who might welcome the opportunity to serve, once again, as a mother.

"Your grandmother called your brother and sisters 'punks,'" I say to Penny, folding the letter back into its envelope. "Maybe that was her opinion of teenagers."

"She could be tough. She insisted on manners. I minded her," Penny says.

"What did your father think of her?"

"He respected her. He listened to her. I remember my mother once complaining that whatever her mother wanted from Glenn she got, the implication being that my dad didn't favor Mom in the same way."

Now Penny pulls from Hattie's file box an atlas, published in 1942, with Germany spread all over Europe, the occupied countries outlined in dotted lines. Grandma Hattie harshly criticized the capitulating Swedes, Penny remembers. Her grandma, one hundred percent Norwegian, never forgave her own country's quislings. She was always so proud that the Norwegian Resistance fought the Germans to the end of the war.

⊘ ⊘ ⊘

The prize for naming the Boyd's coffee bird was the black-and-white TV in Hattie's living room. Penny remembers sitting with her grandma to watch Lawrence Welk, *As the World Turns*, and finally the show that seemed to pull her grandma to the edge of the couch. The man in a suit with a microphone beneath his pencil-thin mustache pointed at Penny herself sitting next to her grandma and shouted, "Would you like to be Queen for a Day?"

Grandma Hattie watched *Queen for a Day* faithfully, and Penny tells me that it was during one of these afternoon episodes, perhaps after the sign-off—"This is Jack Bailey, wishing we could make every woman a queen for every single day"—her grandma revealed that she too had once been a "Queen for a Day." In the box of her effects and files, I found a clipping that mentioned Hattie Spangberg had won the title, but there were no details.

When I ask Penny what her grandmother had told her about being on the program, Penny says, "She never told me very much. She just mentioned it once or twice when I was a little girl. When I asked her if she was on TV, she said no, it was before that." *Queen for a Day* premiered in 1945 as a radio show in New York. A few months later, the show moved to Los Angeles and became a nationally syndicated television show in 1956, three years after the Spangbergs moved to Kennewick. Most likely, Grandma Hattie was a contestant on the radio program. Unfortunately, the recordings of all those radio shows have been destroyed. The show demanded that each contestant bare her soul and reveal her losses and her need to win. Penny felt sorry for the women who registered zero on the applause meter. Grandma Hattie seemed to know who was going to win every time. By today's standards, the show traded on the exploitation of human misery. Was such public humiliation more acceptable in the 1950s? Why did Hattie Spangberg endure it? Perhaps so soon after the war, when women fell back to the anonymity and isolation of a domestic sphere, *Queen for a Day*, a show about women for women, served a cultural purpose: to acknowledge their hardships and validate their abilities to cope. Given a stage, the suffering of these women became stories that connected the audience and contestants alike. All were recognized before one was chosen.

Grandma Hattie was chosen. What did she ask for, I wonder, as a contestant on *Queen for a Day*, and what did she win? Hattie mentioned in a newspaper column some years later that she had found her life "pretty rough at times." But Jack Bailey would insist on specifics.

Did she say, "My name is Hattie Spangberg, and I live in Pasadena with my husband, George. He's my second husband. My first died many years ago back in North Dakota."

"I'm so sorry, dear. But you found George," Jack Bailey may have replied.

"Oh, yes, he was my high school sweetheart."

"Well, that's just fine and you moved out to sunny California to get away from those North Dakota winters?"

"Yes, and to care for my oldest son, who has been ill."

"But before the show you told us that he is being taken care of and that you wanted something quite different if you indeed become our Queen for a Day."

"Yes, I want help moving because someone needs me."

I imagine Hattie Spangberg made her case based not on need for herself but on family necessity: A worried father, her son-in-law, the newspaper he founded at war with two other local papers. The libel suits piling up. A community divided into friends or foes. Her daughter, a mother again at forty-two, ten steps behind her three teenage children, a woman pulled too many ways, too distracted and worried to care full time for a new child.

"I know how to keep a home," Hattie Spangberg may have said. And I imagine she felt that this new grandchild deserved a safe place, what the *New York Times* columnist Roger Cohen would call a "world of unfiltered experience, of things felt rather than thought through, of the world in its beauty absorbed before it is understood, of patterns and sounds that lodge themselves in some indelible place in the psyche and call out across the years."

◊ ◊ ◊

That "world" would be her grandmother's house. Penny mentions that her mother dropped her off every Friday, "with no explanation." Then the cat followed her up to the attic where she looked for fabric remnants. She laid them out on the rough plank floor of the attic and decided what to make, clothes for her dolls perhaps and many times a cape worthy of a queen that day, terry cloth a child's ermine and red velvet.

There were stacks of *McCall's* magazines and a pair of scissors. *McCall's* had paper dolls and cut-out clothes. Her grandmother gave her sheets of paper on which she drew paper-doll dresses and blouses. There were yellow manila envelopes provided by Grandma into which Penny sorted her paper dolls and their ensembles. Stacked and saved at Grandma's house, the envelopes never went home.

The two Siamese cats, Tongo and Mitzi, came with restrictions. Be good to the cats, her grandmother insisted. Tongo with a perfect half-circle kink in his tail, where Penny would tie a red ribbon and watch the cat turn the corner into the living room, its tail the last to disappear, the ribbon half a count behind. Penny remembers just enough of her own mischievousness to warrant rules. Don't chase the chickens. No trespassing in the cookie room. Careful with the dishes. Put things back where you found them.

The cookie room was most tempting. Penny says Grandma Hattie was a wonderful baker, her special joy and talent, famous among family and friends for her Norwegian cookies. Every September, she set up shop and the baking continued into December when she fashioned cookie platters to give as Christmas gifts. The baking was serious work indeed and Penny had to mind and follow her grandma's instructions to the letter. Clean hands. No tasting. The mixing just so. When they were finished with baking and the cleaning up each day, Penny was allowed to choose one cookie from the cookie room.

Only one! How to decide? There were *fatigmann*, made with cream and brandy; butter cookies squeezed into shapes from a press; *krumkaker*, a waffle cookie, cooked on a special griddle and rolled into a cone; *pepperkaker*, a spicy ginger cookie; *kringla*, or spritz cookies, a rope cookie twisted in a loop, baked, then one end dipped in chocolate; double cookies, with a layer of jam in between; *kokosmak-roner*, a coconut macaroon; *goro*, a square cookie, cooked on a special griddle and flavored with cardamom and cream; *sandbakkelse*, or sand cakes, cookie dough pressed into tiny tart pans, baked, and then filled with a sweet filling; rolled cookies, cut into shapes with cookie cutters, then frosted and decorated; and rosettes, deep-fried with a special iron to create the flower shape, then dusted with powdered sugar. Woe to anyone who entered the cookie room without permission; such trespasses Grandma Hattie threatened with a smack from her big wooden spoon. No one disobeyed.

❧　❧　❧

Before dinner Penny peeled vegetables, the carrots and potatoes and turnips, the kitchen warm, the window fogged from the kettle or the dishwater, the light diffuse from orange to brown, the leaves turning, then bright reflected off the first snows. Grandma Hattie would cut into pumpkins and Penny would scrape the seeds out and spread them on a cookie sheet to dry. The kitchen served as the staging ground for winter. A cold room beside the garage kept their provisions, Grandpa George in his apron before a big flat table where he would roll out *rullepolse* or mix the pieces into his sausage mix or roll out *lefse*.

Then to spring and the "windfall light." The yard was Penny's garden. A swing hung from a clothesline pole, birds singing, the robins and chickadees she hears still in Iowa. There was searching as well as wonder and a gathering at all times, the things she could see and hear, but

also a gathering of herself in this place, where she fit, what
she contributed, where the boundaries were and the play
allowed inside those boundaries. She drew her world
on sheets of paper and populated it with cats. Large and
warm and flour-dusted, her grandmother moved slowly
and indomitably through that world. Her grandfather
made things and took Penny in his Buick to deliver coffee and cookies to the pressmen at the *Tri-City Herald* each
morning, who would stop to talk a moment, the men in
ink-stained aprons beside the huge cylinders of the hot
type press. As the deadline approached, the racket of the
Linotype machines increased.

Penny remembers the homing pigeons Grandpa George
raised in a shed in the backyard. How they would soar and
tumble in the blue sky above the yard before returning to
their coop in the evening, where Grandpa George would
tend to them with feed and excelsior. And how sad were
the newly hatched squabs, naked and baldheaded, with
big round eyes and wide open beaks. Such helplessness.
Would they ever fly?

When the morning arrived, "white with dew,"
Grandma Hattie sent Penny to look for eggs laid in secret
corners of the garden. She would search behind the roses,
taking great care not to be thorned, between the raised
beds, along the strawberry rows, and under the chrysan-
themums. "Find them all. We don't want our chickens to go
broody!" "Broody" a word Penny murmured for its double
o's, the melancholy sound, what she would feel alone in
her room on Sunday evening at home. Here in the backyard, however, she could do something about it. She could
find the hidden eggs and set them into a basket, outsmart-
ing her grandmother's menagerie of chickens: the Arau-
cana's blue eggs and feathers made for Sunday hats, the
brown eggs of the Plymouth Rock, the light brown eggs of
the Brahma, kicking up dust with its feathered toes despite

its good manners, the white of the Jersey Giant, and the rare brown speckled eggs of the Welsummer.

Resolute, an eye out for the rooster, a Rhode Island Red, the r's like his crowing at dawn, Penny set the chickens aflutter, rummaged in their roost boxes, and searched the fence line, stopping only to step aside for the Polish chicken. What hand designed her red wattles and black body, her topknot of feathers in gold and silver, so luxuriant and sweeping she can hardly see where she's going? Penny thought of her mother and wondered if this chicken would find a place to lay its eggs. Years later, Penny remembers her grandmother called that elegant chicken "Top Hanna."

Then there was the gathering of fruits and vegetables. As each came ready, Penny helped Grandma and Grandpa pick the beans and peas and raspberries and strawberries. And then she would help weed the flowerbeds and the rock garden, listening to her grandmother name the flowers, the tea and floribundas, the Queen Elizabeth and Peace roses.

○   ○   ○

Each spring, Penny replants her grandmother's flowers in her own garden, her memory tilled and tended and blossoming anew. In our backyard, we have a purple clematis and a blue; both once climbed her grandmother's back fence. At the west edge of our deck, the Japanese iris, spirea, and crab apple; to the north, yellow daisies, salvia and anemones, iris and bee balm, violets and carnations; to the east, roses and bleeding heart and hydrangea; and the dogwood, the flowers representing the cross, the rusty nails, and the crown of thorns, Grandma Hattie explained; and finally, a rhododendron, planted twenty-five years ago. The rhody has survived Iowa winters and pruning, and each spring its pink blossoms are among the first to remind

Penny of Grandma Hattie's own rhododendron, transplanted from Pasadena, California, its root ball wrapped in burlap for the trip one thousand miles north, to care for a little girl in Kennewick, Washington.

◊　◊　◊

There were eggs and sweet rolls and coffee Sunday mornings. Grandma Hattie hurried Penny into the clean dress hung in the closet all weekend and buckled on her Mary Janes. She brushed Penny's hair while Grandpa George warmed up the big Buick in the driveway. Church started at nine.

What must it have been like for Penny to go home with her mom and dad on Sunday after church, the house too quiet or static charged, the impending Sunday dinner, one sister away at school, one sister married and gone, an older brother in college but home in the summer and living in the basement and eating alone? There was tension as well as sorrow in her house. Her father struggled to keep his business afloat. There were mysterious phone calls and raised voices; there were doors slammed and doors kept locked. There were tears and arguments and silence, and her mother who stayed awake late into the night. In her room, Penny tried to survive in that landscape of anxiety and loneliness. But she had a safe haven with her Grandma Hattie.

What was a grandmother to do, besides caretaking? Perhaps her son-in-law the newspaper publisher, who so admired Grandma Hattie's words of encouragement, asked her to help the readers of the *Tri-City Herald* as well. Perhaps a Sunday column in the women's section was just what she needed to spread the good word. If so, she got her wish.

On February 4, 1962, Hattie launched herself as a newspaper columnist; her nom de plume was Grandmother

Greene. In her files, I found the draft of her initial column, typed on her upright Underwood. "I'm a Grandmother with a 'Treasure Chest' full of gold 'nuggets' that I have been gathering—one here, one there—since I was a little girl sixty years ago. Some brought me Joy and Laughter, some have given me Faith, Courage, and Inspiration, and have helped me smooth the rough spots in the Highway of Life." The last line of her column reads, "Thank God for emergencies." I think there was crisis enough to keep her busy.

Then her weekly sortie began, a kind of "good word" counteroffensive, aimed as much at family, I'm sure, as the newspaper audience. A Christian soldier onward, she pounded out her columns for eighty-six weeks. An advocate for scripture, church, teachers, prayer, gardens, family, home, and a good and godly attitude, the common road we all travel, she worked hard at bringing forth the word.

At times, however, I can sense a little frustration. In a column published August 12, 1962, she quotes Joseph Fort Newton, "We can do anything for one day." Where Newton's quote leaves off and Grandmother Greene's commentary starts up remains ambiguous, but I can hear her when she says, "Suppose we make up our minds to be happy, *Just for a Day*. To make the world over to suit us is a large order . . . So *Just for Today*, let us be agreeable, responsive, cheerful, charitable; be our best, walk safely, praise people for what they do, not criticize them for what they cannot do. And if we find fault, let us forgive and forget." Whomever Grandma Hattie intended as the target audience, she let Grandmother Greene take the aim.

Her last column was published December 29, 1963. She quotes a series of wishes by W. Waldemar W. Argow, a minister in the 1930s, and I can't help but think that either Hattie Spangberg had exhausted her energy for this work or she felt a debilitating sorrow at that moment in her own life. Grandpa George was ill and would die the next year. The tension surrounding her children and grandchildren and now great-grandchildren remained palpable. John F. Kennedy was only a month in the grave and perhaps Grandma Hattie's own optimism and cheer suffered along with the country's. "What dare I wish for that this year may bring me? A few sincere friends who understand my loneliness yet remain faithful because of my silence." The column ends with the wish "That as my little day closes, [I] do feel the encircling arms of 'the love that will not let me go.'" It sounds ominous, and she writes no more.

In 1963 I was a senior in high school. Ten years later, Penny and I announced to her parents that we were getting married. I don't remember when she told her grandma, but I imagine Hattie's words of encouragement and warm embrace that would call Penny back to years of warm kitchens and dusty attics. Her parents wished us well, but only later did I learn that Penny's father had been actively recruiting other suitors for her, young men who worked at the *Tri-City Herald*. Perhaps I made a less than favorable impression at that awkward first dinner. Penny was having none of it, however. She said her father listened when Grandma Hattie spoke to him in my favor. Perhaps this was one of the last things she wanted. What Hattie wanted, I know by now, Hattie got, and Penny's father stopped his recruiting. By the time Penny and I were married, her grandma was very ill with diabetes, her toes gone and her body failing. The last time we visited her, she was in pain, incoherent, as Penny tried to soothe her. Then Grandma Hattie saw me standing at the foot of her bed, sat up and said, "Hi, Jim." It was clear. She was my advocate. Now after all these years, she still gives me her granddaughter's hand to care for, and we lay her back down in the closing day.

Stations, 1979

Posing

Our first stop, Crete. Here in a red blouse and white pants, her long blond hair swept back by the Aeolian wind, Penny stands on the balcony next to the vertical Hotel Kronos sign. Our room is on the third floor next to the *e* in hotel. Although hardly begun, our trip has been long already, night flights and bad taxis all the way to Heraklion. Here she is standing before the ruins of Knossos, relaxed and young before three thousand years' worth of stone. She looks newly released from the labyrinth, free of the Minotaur, the dolphins leaping in celebration over her head.

Later that evening we search the streets near our hotel for a restaurant and find one at last, though the outside tables are empty, the chairs leaned up. "Jim, it looks closed. I'm starving," Penny says, and grabs my sleeve as if to hold herself up.

"I'm sorry," I say, turning this way and that, searching for something, knowing this is my fault. "Too many photos." And then from the doorway, a man waves us into the kitchen. We speak no Greek, but he gestures to the pots still bubbling on the stove. We bend to the fragrance of eggplant and calamari. He hands us each a plate and we dish up and walk outside, a candle now lit on one table. A long

way from home, I imagine our wings. We are in Europe
for eight weeks to wander from Greece to England: a survival test perhaps for a young married couple, or maybe
just my desire to lead my wife on an adventure. A decade
earlier I had traveled through Europe playing basketball
for the Gillette All-Stars, and I suggested to Penny that we
could retrace those steps and add a few of our own. She
was reluctant. Eight weeks?

"We'll find our way," I might have said. Not so sure
tonight, we sit at this restaurant beside a quiet street on a
warm evening. We dine alone except for the cats of Crete,
scenting the legs of our table. Feral, some with their tails
broken, they stay just out of Penny's reach when she offers
a morsel and circle us as quiet as the wind through the
tamarisk.

"Calamari in Crete," she says. "How delicious."

Here she is on a promontory overlooking the city of
Rhodes. Penny leans against a bench. In the background at
the harbor's edge, I imagine the Colossus, a wonder of the
world, spanning the harbor's entry, though in this photo,
Penny stands as tall. In another, she waits in miniature a
long way from the camel I asked her to pose next to, ladder
and saddle at the ready as I back toward the edge of a cliff,
an incremental leaving. "Please don't," she calls out. "That
scares me." Trying to center her in my viewfinder, I stop,
a rail bumping my hip, and look over my shoulder down
at the tops of trees, the thread of a road and its black cars
vanishing into the city. I shift, quickly, a few steps closer to
Penny and focus the camera on her smile. Here, in another
photo, she poses before a Greek Orthodox church at the
end of a long climb on a hot day, the sun bleaching the
stone streets of Rhodes.

"What prompted our trip?" I ask her now.

"We needed to wander," she says. Yes, we wandered on
the bus to Archangelos and past idle donkey taxis. There

are five saddled up in the picture and twelve drivers sitting along a white stucco wall and smoking. Up the steep path we walk past the lace sellers spreading their wares on white stone, until finally, after three hundred stone steps we arrive at the Monastery of Tsambika: 339 meters above the turquoise water and white sand of Tsambika Bay. The view is as breathless as we are. When we try to enter the monastery chapel, an old woman steps in front of Penny and holds up a square yard of wool cloth. No shorts or pants for women it seems. For a drachma, the woman provides a skirt, her knuckles as polished as olive wood. She cinches the belt around Penny's waist. Penny gasps, eyes wide before exhaling, a moment of suffering and penance she must accept before we enter the holy space. Penny remembers the cobblestone mosaics of the floor. I remember the wheel of beeswax candles hanging from the dark ceiling, the mystery of heaven in shadows above the holy gilt of the walls' frescos.

Eros Hotel

We have no idea how to leave Athens gracefully. In our hotel on Omonia Square, the clerk writes "train station" in Greek on a card and hails a taxi for us. The driver, a young man, dark hair and dark glasses, his collar turned up, points us toward his backseat and glances at the card as we load our suitcases into his trunk. We climb in. He drives off, lights a cigarette, and joins the first traffic jam he can find. Levering the gear shift into park, the engine and meter still running, he gets out to chat and share a glass of ouzo with friends he spots in a sidewalk café. Terrific. Here we sit, stranded.

Nothing seems straightforward in Greece. We've spent two days crisscrossing Athens trying to leave, having discovered ferry tickets are available only at the east end of town, the exit tax stamp, of course, only in the west. Now we're stalled in the middle, the train station far in our future and the ferry waiting in Patras. Hadn't we filled in the blanks and completed the forms, walked up to and around the Acropolis and the sisters, eaten good Greek food, tipped all the waiters, and traveled by bus clear to Delphi to consult the oracle, trekking uphill until we found the outdoor amphitheater where Penny sat thirty-five rows up on a stone seat in the sun? She watched me locate the one spot onstage where she could hear me tell her how glad I was that we had reached the center of the earth together. I whispered and still my voice carried.

"This guy's not coming back," Penny says.

"We're out of here," I say. Wasting no time, we climb out the back door, open the trunk lid, and haul our suitcases free, traffic honking fore and aft. As we maneuver our way between the cars, the taxi driver knocks back his ouzo and shouts. I turn to salute him in English, my Apollonian pledge a mix of raspberry and the promise never to forget him or his dented taxi.

At the ferry landing in Patras, hard-won tickets allowed us passage and nothing else, an overnight trip on the deck of the *Appia*, where we found a corner out of the wind to eat tuna fish and bread and sleep surrounded by our baggage, Penny's head on my shoulder. Destination Corfu.

Six hours later, we stand before a tourist booth only to discover there's not a hotel to be found in Corfu Town. Oh fine, Penny's expression seems to say, the air between us silent except for a distant seagull's cry. Tired, exasperated, at a loss, I pick up our bags, which now feel twice as heavy. "Oh, wait," the woman in the tourist booth holds a hand up. "There's one room in the Eros Hotel in Benitses, twelve kilometers south. Take the green bus through the olive groves along the Ionian Sea."

We stand the whole way, still bleary-eyed from our crossing the night before. You are lucky, the hotel manager tells us, as we fill in our information and show her our passports, for the hotel is booked for a wedding today and the reception tonight in the hotel's *taverna*. Your room is the last one left. At the top of the stairs, our room is neat and tidy with a balcony that overlooks the calm, blue sea, a wooden dock pointing straight out toward the haze of a distant island. We lean over our railing to see the *taverna* directly below us, happy to have found a place to unpack and a quiet moment.

Maybe it's the sea air or the motor scooter we hire that morning to ride through the streets of Benitses, through the olive groves and out along the white beach. Maybe it's the afternoon swimming in the bay, the sun reflecting everywhere off the white stucco. Maybe it's the early dinner of tomatoes and cucumber and fish, a glass or two of *retsina*, a moment to commiserate with each other for our twenty-four hours of bad taxis and second-class trains and the steel deck of a spartan ferry and local buses and so much walking uphill. Maybe it's Penny's sitting by herself on our balcony, pensive a moment as the sun drops red into the Ionian Sea, how she holds the hair off the back of her neck with one hand and stands and moves toward the bed and touches it, as if it is the most comfortable place she has found on this whole island, rose petals left by the management spilling onto the floor and our mosquito netting yet to be untied. Maybe for all this, we decide to put the name of our hotel to the test. The guitars have started up downstairs and the laughter, including our own. The serenade has begun.

I don't remember much after that. Not a sound. I don't remember the music or the smashing of plates or the money toast or the cheers. Penny remembers waking at four when the music finally stopped. I was as tired that evening as the man I discovered the next morning. The sun just up, I wandered into the *taverna* to look for coffee and there he was, the father of the bride or perhaps her uncle, sitting cockeyed and fast asleep in his chair, his collar undone, mouth open, hair mussed, and still in his hand the handkerchief he must have held to dance the *Kalamatiano*, round and round until he could dance no more. Among the empty glasses and cans and plates strewn here and there, the flowers slumped in their vases, the bandstand empty, the bride and groom long departed, the evening's last reveler stays behind and snores.

Let him sleep. Penny and I rose early and packed to leave the Eros Hotel, a lucky find, tested and true to its name.

Our Reservations

The strategy we used as we arrived at each station: exit the train, find a locker to store our bags, scout for hotel rooms available through booths or advertised on kiosks at the station, then stand in line to make a reservation to leave a few days later: two couchette tickets, please, second class.

Those were our best-laid plans executed in train stations, the nexus of human turmoil, where nobody lives but where much business is done, these stone and glass and steel cathedrals to engines and movement, and the possibility of greener grass. Great wonderful machines on fixed rails like parallel streams of light pointing toward Denmark and Paris. Such urgings, desire, yearning for someplace new or home. Dreamtime on a schedule.

But after weeks of train rides, we were both sleep deprived, bags stickered with every place we'd been, our equilibrium rocky after so much movement, so many transitions and comings and goings and negotiations, the fares, the crowds, the couchettes with six bunks, each five feet long and stacked three to a side. Old ladies who snored, claimed the bottom bunks, and slept with their bags of onions; once a young Swede disrobed to his skivvies in front of us all, and leapt into his middle bunk as if to stop a goal. Lights out. Marking our breath, the wheels on the track kept time, ticking in a traveler's metronome.

Penny asks if I remember the elderly woman on the train to Switzerland, the one who sat across from us, the one with the big diamond ring. She had a wallet full of hundred-dollar bills she counted with her thumbs, purse open. We tried to mind our own business. Finally, she said something to me in French, and I responded with what little French I had, "*Pardonnez-moi, je ne parle pas français.*" To which she responded once again in French.

"What did she say?" I asked Penny.

"What language do you speak?" Penny answered.

"Sorry, English," I said turning back to the woman who had finished arranging her finances.

"Then let us use English," she said, adopting us for the remainder of the train trip as her confidants. We had brought our lunch with us and spoke quietly. She thought we were Canadian. No, no, we're American, we explained, but she decided to count us as friends anyway. How she talked, this elderly woman from New York City who traveled each year to Switzerland to see family who had survived the Holocaust. "We are Jewish, you see, and lived in Berlin. My father moved us in the late 1930s to Amsterdam. When the Nazis threatened Holland, he moved us to New York.

"He was a smart man," was her refrain thirty-five years after the war. "A smart man."

⊘   ⊘   ⊘

But finally we needed to rest, I in the top bunk and Penny beneath me, out of sight but within reach, two taps in the springs to remind me she was still there. I would reach over the edge to find her, hand in hand in our nighttime journey. And then we slept. Much needed, given our Paris destination and my stumbling in French, Penny coaching me as we pulled into the Gare du Nord. *"Excusez-moi, Madame. Avez-vous une réservation pour McKean?"*

"You speak French far better than I do," I said, but Penny insisted I place the call. She would explain years later that she was too worn out to unravel a tangle of French on the telephone, that maybe the hotel manager would take slow pity on me, an obvious beginner.

"Say it back to me," she said as I pushed the French coins into the public telephone and dialed the hotel's number written on a scrap of paper.

"Hotel Navarone," the woman's voice said and I repeated my phrase. We had made these arrangements at home months before, planning in the fifth year of our marriage a first trip to Europe together, and now the woman hesitated, papers shuffling in the background, or was it static on the line, and said, *"Non."*

"No?" I said aloud. Penny's eyes widened. *"McKean? Avez-vous une réservation pour McKean?"* I pronounced again. Oh please, let me sound a little French, oh please, let my syllables roll, let my tongue elide, let the accents fall peacefully.

"Non," she said.

"No? Oh man," I said to the telephone and then to the desperate air, *"Sacré bleu!"* in cartoon French, holding my hand over the phone and glancing at Penny who looked on the verge of tears. Once more I tried, *"S'il vous plait, Madame. Avez-vous une réservation pour McKean?"*

"McKean, McKean . . . un moment. Ah, oui . . . trois nuits."

She gave directions I didn't understand as I said *"Merci"* over and over. After a long night on the train, it was more suspense than we needed. Then we discovered our beloved Madame was stingy with every aspect of her small hotel, with greetings, coffee, bread, storage, linen, and bonhomie. But we were in Paris and in the Pigalle district. We relished the Art Nouveau metro stops and even the razzing I took from *les filles de joie,* who sat behind their tavern's open Dutch door as I walked back to our hotel each morning with sweet rolls and a newspaper under my arm. Maybe it was my red face as I tried to look straight ahead or the fact that I stood six foot nine. No matter. They would not be ignored. Each time I walked by, the laughter and catcalls grew more intense. On our last morning in Paris, I knew I had to say something, make some gesture. Stopping before them, I turned and bowed—fell really— over the half door, sweeping my hat through the cigarette smoke and morning perfume and exclaimed in my newly gargled French, *"Bonjour, mesdames et mademoiselles. Comment allez-vous?"* Oh, what celebration so early in the morning! Boas and dressing gowns and cheers erupted. I had arrived, less a spectator and more a bit player, whose audition landed him a small role on the Pigalle stage.

A Word for the French Gentleman Who Watched My Wife All Evening from His Table Next to Us at the Lido in Paris

Now that you ask, we've been three weeks traipsing through timetables, carrying too many bags, a change for every occasion—tonight for instance, a coat and tie, slacks and shoes for me, a long dress and heels for her—dressed up to stand hours in line for the Lido, an evening at the end of threads unwound clear from the labyrinth of Knossos.

We've ridden the decks of ferries and bunked in railroad cars with ancient Italian aunts and their onions. We've turned in circles, stunned by Michelangelo's ceiling. We've waited and smiled and pointed and eaten what we thought we ordered and gestured at taxi drivers who charged us full fare to drop us halfway. Imagine us, our arms hung with suitcases, anxious to find our voice in Greek, Italian, the French for "pardon me." Imagine us street after street, skirting boxes of wilted produce and stray dogs, and then imagine us finding the right peach at last, its scent on our hands, before the narrowest alley opens onto a sunlit piazza, its coffee and pigeons, its church all mosaics and uneven floors. Yes. For weeks we've carried the freight of our expectations. And now that we're at intermission, my wife off to freshen up—yes, that is she turning back to wave—I'm glad you've asked, for I can tell you the management has seated us so close to the stage, I can hear the Bluebell girls chuff in their headgear and wings, high kicking in "*Du Jerk a Gogo*," the bruises plain beneath their net stockings. How the juggler sweated beneath his spinning plates, how the poodles walked their handlers on two legs up the stairs and through their hoops, the "Dancing Waters" number soaking our cuffs, the ice skaters on edge, the crooner hedging his vibrato. Thank you. We've worked hard to dress up to watch hard work all dressed up. We've found the one-liners in French lost on us but the pratfalls as clear as the songs of love. And yes, now that you ask, we've hauled ourselves a long way to sit here, to imagine Josephine Baker or Edith Piaf singing only to us from that very stage—yes, a long way on foot, hand in hand, to sip watery drinks at a miniature table and no, please, my French *is* terrible, and yes, the show is everything I'd hoped for and the band splendid and yes, my wife will be back momentarily after all this and under no circumstances may you ask her to dance.

Wash Day

Lovely neutral Zurich, Switzerland. In *Frommer's* we have found a place to stay with the nuns in their convent. Thirty years later, the convent has long since dissolved in fact and almost in memory, except for one clean moment. A nun takes Penny's elbow and ushers her into the office. I hold our bags and peer up the stairs toward the celestial light. Are we penitents? Have we been saved?

Now we cannot remember the name of their order. Let's call them the Sisters of the Vinegar Wash, maybe Sisters of the Alcohol Wipes? No bargain, this room I lift my eyes toward, clean, austere, the air mote-free, what we needed after the Pigalle district of Paris, an American couple traipsing four weeks through the fallen world to arrive in a dust cloud at the convent doorstep. Our Lady of the Wire Rims? I haul our bags step by step up the stairs to a room with windows on three sides, big enough for a dormitory but empty except for us, our bags at our feet. There are easy chairs and two twin beds, one at each end of the room. The Perpetual Order of Separate Beds and Safe Distances?

Who were these nuns? We can't find any record of them now. They wore blue-gray habits, white wimples that pinched their faces, their eyes bright blue, electric. Sisters of the Key Ring when we register in the office downstairs. Maybe Our Mother of the Surcharge, as the francs begin to add up, but we don't care. Tired this evening, we're willing to pay a little extra for towels, for soap and Kleenex, for clean fresh-from-the-line, sun-dried cotton sheets.

The chairs are as stuffed as uncles and the beds so comfortable Penny wakes the next morning and thinks she's home. I'm thinking of Richard Wilbur's poem where the "astounded soul / Hangs for a moment bodiless and simple." We are suspended in light through the banks of windows, lifted by the sweet smell of coffee rising from somewhere beneath us, the rattle of dishes, water running, and perhaps for such a good night's sleep and clean simple morning, Penny's own soul might call out as well, "Oh, let there be nothing on earth but laundry." When we checked in the night before, she had noticed washers and dryers tucked into a back room on the first floor, a folding table, running water, the scent of soap and rising steam. She had asked if we were free to use the laundry. Yes, the nun said, who pulled the handle on her adding machine, counted out change and turned the book toward Penny so that she might log us in.

Now after days of railcars, after stations, after walking a long way in our soiled clothes and tired shoes to get here and sleep all night, we can lift ourselves from clean sheets and down comforters, and spend the morning at our wash. Given this chance to unpack, Penny throws a pillowcase full of clothes over her shoulder and descends the stairs to the blessed laundry room, two washing machines, two dryers slightly elevated, and a table where the liturgy of sorting might be performed, blouses and jeans, socks and shorts, underwear and jackets, her hands warm and ready in anticipation of water and soap.

The holy wash cycles, the heat from the dryers, the sanctified steam, the starch returned to cotton and then the sorting and refolding, but not so fast. Perhaps she was not so free after all. She thought she had permission to use the machines, but never assumed for free. Perhaps the good sister, intent on her ledger last night, misunderstood Penny's request or dismissed it, for filling the doorway now the "heaviest" of nuns, livid in her wimple, barks at Penny in German and points at the stack of folded laundry and sweeps the air as if to cleanse the sight before her.

"*Nein, Nein,*" the sister repeats after a long harangue in German, the content unclear but the tone unmistakable.

Deferential, respectful of the nun's authority and a bit stunned at being caught off guard, Penny explains how she had asked permission, but her English and her folded clothes seem to anger the sister more. Our Lady of Rage?

"You must pay," the sister finally says in broken English. Penny reaches into her purse, as the nun steps closer, shaking her finger and repeating even louder, "You must pay. You must pay." Now we are fallen from grace. Now we are considered thieves. At that moment, Penny understands that a few francs will never satisfy what this nun is calling due or heal the source of her anger. At that moment, Penny realizes that in her life she has suffered too much anger from those around her who demanded some measure of pain and fear, the exact figures notwithstanding.

"Enough, enough," Penny says, her voice suddenly a chill in this warm humid room, and waves the paper money at the sister. "I asked permission and I said I would pay. Now I will pay you. Now I am paying."

At this the sister steps back, baffled perhaps by Penny's conjugations, but aware, I'm sure, of her tone. This sister, red-faced and silent, grasping for that "difficult balance" between love and collecting the rent. The blond tourist, young and slender, is tougher than she expected. Penny lays the francs on the folding table. "Take it," she says.

"And let us take ourselves out of here," Penny says to me as we pack our fresh clothes and head out the door. We deposit our suitcases at the train station and spend an afternoon on the good ship *Limmat*, following the sun across the clean, blue waters of Lake Zurich.

Lost in Amsterdam

Penny and I needed to stay close, I thought, and we did as the cities scrolled by, within earshot or sight, sleeping one above the other on night trains and walking the rest of the way through Europe, hand in hand along the cobbled streets.

But arrivals were complicated. As we stepped off the train one morning in Rome's Termini Station, Penny said she was tired, and we found a seat in a row of empty chairs at one end of the station, so she could sit with our luggage and wait for me to buy tickets to our next destination. I wasn't long but when I returned, an Italian gentleman, well dressed, brilliantined, was sitting next to Penny, leaning toward her on his elbow to whisper in her ear. Hands folded in her lap and sitting very straight, she stared ahead as if trying to concentrate on an impossibly difficult exam question.

"No, no," I said, and sat with a flourish in the chair on the other side of the man, and leaned into him and opened a newspaper to let him in on the news, my elbow just below his chin, and said, "No, no, you're not staying here, pal," at which he stood, gathered himself, adjusted his tailored jacket, and left us to our holiday in Rome.

In Munich, we arrived late to see the German police beat a vagrant who was sleeping on a bench in the train station. I searched the kiosks for a room. It was past midnight. Penny stood by our bags only to be approached by a small, elderly woman who said to her in English, "You're not thinking about staying in the train station. It's not safe. Come stay with me." Nothing felt safe. Hotel number in hand finally, I walked back to Penny as the two policemen rolled the vagrant off the bench with a thud and handcuffed him. Lucky again to find a room for the night, we left the next day.

We survived every day tired by the end, tested by the crowds and language, tested by all that was unfamiliar to us. Up 650 steps to the dome of St. Peter's, for example, and down single file on a hot day behind a man with a wooden leg. Or riding the Metro for an hour in Paris to

find good local food, or meandering through the graves of
Pére Lachaise. And too, there were things we still didn't
know about each other. Penny had stood her ground in
Zurich. That didn't surprise me. What I didn't see, however, behind such defiance and steel, was how fragile her
sense of safety might be. Growing up in a dysfunctional
family, she understood anger. After such outbursts, alone
in her room, the door locked from the inside, she felt lost
and sad. On our travels, she and I were discovering how
to be close to each other and what space to allow, and how
to keep each other's company. By the time we reached
Amsterdam, I thought I knew what those distances were,
even in a strange landscape. But storm clouds gathered
that day in the dark water of a canal.

We found a room some distance from the train station.
We left our bags in the station and walked the mile or so
to our hotel, a room one flight up above a butcher's shop
on a small back street beside a canal. Tidy, with windows
overlooking a backyard, the room would be our home for
one night. Penny said she wanted to take a nap. I told her
I would walk back to the train station for our luggage and
tickets and wouldn't be long. But I was wrong about that.
The lines at the train station meandered for blocks. When
I finally inched my way to my first ticket window, I was
informed my request for passage to Copenhagen must be
placed at a different window, that this was the domestic
line and if I wouldn't mind finding the end of the foreign
line somewhere around the corner down the hall out into
the street. Then there was a line for a couchette, another
hour, and by the time I retrieved our bags from the locker
and schlepped them the mile back to our room, trying not
to forget how to get there, with only a wrong turn or two,
several hours had passed.

When I turned down our street and saw the butcher
shop, it felt like I was being watched for. Children were

playing on the sidewalk and retrieved their ball as soon as they saw me. The butcher looked up and out his window and stopped his work. Someone was sweeping. Cars and a bicycle rolled by. Standing outside the shop, a man sold flowers from a cart. He looked at me and for some reason I thought he knew me. It's as if his eyes took hold of my elbow and drew me to his cart, gently, suggesting flowers would save the day, a day I didn't know was at risk: carnations and rosebuds, bouquets wrapped in wire and soaking in his buckets. "These?" I asked, and he nodded yes.

As soon as I opened the door, I could see she had been crying. She spoke in a rush. "Where have you been? I thought something had happened to you. I fell asleep and when I woke you weren't there and I walked down to the street but no one spoke English and the butcher and his wife just waved at me. I even walked all the way back to the train station, but I couldn't find you. I thought you were gone." Now I was lost.

Thinking back, I realize I had disappeared in her imagination. She was alone, fluent in nothing, abandoned by her language, by me, by fate, by her every resource, and this terrified her. No explanation about lines and delays on my part would help. This was not something I could fix with an explanation. This was something I needed to understand, how we needed to stay in touch in whatever way possible. I needed to stick by her first and wander second, that all her standing up for herself needed backup. Bags on the floor, out of breath from the climb, holding her, I said sorry, sorry, sorry.

Postscript

I have worked hard to explain what happened that day, not to explain it away, but to see it in my own mind, to see her, and to find something to say. And when I did, I wrote her this: "Late in the day I left you sleeping in the last room in town, descended the stairs through the landlord's butcher shop, and returned hours later, haggard by lines, our bags found, our tickets to somewhere crumpled in my pocket. At the corner I bought you flowers, rosebuds not far from bloom, from an old man who must have heard you crying, awake too soon from hard sleep. Maybe you descended the stairs into a strange city, the wind gone cold, and found even your language lost on the butcher who grimaced, wiping his hands on a red-stained towel, or his wife who cradled your arm and waved at the thin street as if calling her children home. If you found nothing more than black water running through an abandoned canal and all bridges away from here empty, then maybe you climbed those stairs again and lay down to listen: a woman's sweeping outside your door, the butcher scraping his block, the calling of an old man who charged me far too little for the roses he pressed in my hand, so I might lay them beside us, so we might leave them tomorrow blooming in a borrowed vase on a clean and polished table."

Dyed-in-the-Wool

Three words from Penny's father was all it took. At her parents' house I remember a chronic tension held in check for the most part, but once just before we left on a date, her father barked an order at her, something thoughtless, inconsequential, tossed off, something controlling and disrespectful at its center. After our year together, I knew my fiancée had a temper, but this time her ignition seemed even quicker. Five foot three, high cheekbones, three-quarters Norwegian with long blond hair she often hid behind, Penny snapped, "Not having it," smacking her hands together, and all the blue in her eyes discharged.

Her father flinched and took two steps back. Bitten, he rubbed his crew cut and looked for the day's paper. Penny turned toward the hall closet. Where did that fury come from? I remember wondering, as she buttoned up her coat and wrapped a scarf firmly beneath her set jaw. "We're leaving," she announced to the air, and we did, out the front door that evening and eventually into our own lives for good.

We have been married thirty-four years, and I still wonder how she musters such fire. She grew up in a family where a balance of will and deference helped her survive much older siblings, an alcoholic mother, and an overbearing, autocratic, and hugely successful father. But some moments tip her balance. She has stood up to me certainly when I demanded she tag along on my fishing trips, for example, or insisted on one unreasonable concession or another. She is certain about her own authority and ready to respond to those who challenge it. Where does that come from? The more I have looked, the more complex and heroic the answers have become.

At first I thought my wife was simply her father's constitutional heir. In 1949, Penny's father purchased a small-town newspaper in the Tri-Cities, Washington, and the printing press rolled on his gumption and the ironclad opinion that his vision of the world made the best sense, fist pounded into palm. His way or the highway, Penny would say, remembering the deference she paid during her growing-up years when her father survived a thirteen-year strike by the typesetters union, libel suits, an anti-trust action, animosity, vilification, and occasional death threats. He wore a suit one day and a typesetting apron the next. He packed a snub-nosed .38, wrote inflammatory columns that got him sued, visited with the pickets from the International Typesetters Union every morning out on the sidewalk, often serving them coffee and donuts, posing with them before the camera and running the picture the next day on the front page of his own paper. He resisted offset printing for years and had one of the last hot-type printing operations in the United States that worked only because he scoured the country for spare parts for his Linotype machines and press. When economics forced a transition to the cold printing process, he sold the newspaper. It was almost as if he couldn't give up the idea that words needed to be cast in metal and pounded into newsprint before they carried any weight.

By the time I had the good fortune to marry his daughter, his last child at home, my father-in-law's career had boiled down to something calmer, though he still believed Armageddon was just around the corner and stored bottled water and gallon tins of potato buds in his crawl space just in case. I had sat through many Sunday dinners and a tribunal or two of Norwegian aunts and grandparents—porcelain teacups balanced in their laps—as well as birthdays and holidays enough with brothers and uncles and cousins and in-laws that I understood a little of my bride's family history. One hundred percent Norwegian, her mother could dead-reckon her way back through Saxrudes and Evinrudes clear to the Norwegian beach Eric the Red must have pushed off from to sail to Greenland, my mother-in-law's maiden name.

The pedigree of Penny's father, however, was more ambiguous, darker, prompting first an intake of breath. "There were some hard ones in that family," Penny's uncle would say each Fourth of July over his burnt hot dog and potato salad. Half condemning, half reverential, he explained how Penny's grandfather drove a mule team and collected garbage, how his father (Penny's great-grandfather) broke his back in an accident and still managed his farm, how one great-uncle survived the Civil War and another one didn't, how another drowned when his wagon rolled into a stream. Those who survived, the family imagined as tough, independent, tenacious, and long on Anglo-Saxon grit. They were men to be feared as well as admired, I believe, their stories told in single syllables with a lowered voice and a nod of the head.

At the center of this mystery stood their father, Job Lee, his name biblical, though family rumor suggests he did unto others as much as the Lord did unto him.

"What was he like?" I asked my mother-in-law once, curious about why, during middle age, he had moved his family from New York State to Wisconsin in the 1850s.

"Lost to the wolves," was her answer, which struck me as odd. My wife's father took care of things, showed up, persisted for years at hard-nosed business, his reputation and successes public enough that even Senator Henry Jackson remarked to Penny as she and I stood in his office in Washington DC, "Your dad, you sure know where he stands."

More bulldog than wolf, my father-in-law never seemed lost. But who was Job Lee? As my wife's great-great-grandfather, what dark contribution might he have bequeathed to us all? Was there something I needed to know, this being my family now as well? Was straight-ahead determination the approach I needed to claim a place at the family picnic? What had I gotten into?

It's better to find out than to live in the dark, I convinced myself, curious or nosy or just tired of my own family's reticence about its past. I looked and looked for what was lost and only rumored, intrigued I must admit, sure that finding words for a family's story—my wife's story in the end—would make it my story as well. I poked around in the archives of Wisconsin counties. I thumbed through cemetery registries and searched the Internet for Job Lee until sure enough, a trace of him showed here and there. And as the archives opened and envelopes arrived in the mail, I discovered to my great surprise a new name—Rachael Cartwright Lee, Job Lee's wife. She kept his house for thirty years and bore him seven sons and one daughter, and in the end, for good reason, she won the day.

The Dunn County Historical Society was generous to send from their *Dunn County History* a brief description of "The Job Lee Family," which verified much of what I had heard over Thanksgiving dinners. Job and Rachael Cartwright Lee had migrated from Berlin, New York, in 1854, and in the early 1860s became residents of Spring Brook, Wisconsin. Their son Joseph died in a wagon accident in 1866. He was thirty-five. Their daughter Martha Jane married a man who was a justice of the peace. Sons Robert and Phillip fought for the North in the Civil War. Robert survived; Phillip did not. The youngest son, Harvey, suffered a back injury in a farming accident and had to move to Eau Claire, Wisconsin, the birthplace of my father-in-law. Another son, David, was a large landowner, and according to family tradition, he served as banker for his brothers' farming enterprises. The article celebrates the Lee family by stating that "all . . . were successful farmers of Spring Brook and between eight of them were thirty-nine surviving children to carry on the good name."

By 1984, the historians of Dunn County had recorded the death dates and burial sites of almost everybody in the family, including Rachael Cartwright Lee who "lies at rest with her offspring in Waneka." But they knew neither the death date nor the burial site for Job Lee. Where had the wolves taken him, I wondered, and why even at family holiday gatherings did I still hear only a *sotto voce* mention of his name? If I looked long enough, maybe I'd find him somewhere in Wisconsin.

Then Google led me to the Jefferson County Historical Society, which had catalogued in its archives, "twenty-two pages of legal documents for Job Lee." When I inquired, they were more than happy to send a copy, at a dollar a page. I expected bills of sale, perhaps deeds or receipts for livestock or crops. After all, Job Lee had sold a farm in New York, brought his family to Wisconsin by ox team and barge on the Erie Canal, and settled in Wisconsin. Maybe there would be a will, something to reveal his thinking. When the envelope came in the mail, it contained twenty-two legal-sized pages handwritten in hasty Spencerian script, the transcriber obviously trying to keep up with deposition after deposition. The pages were difficult to read and amazing to comprehend.

Rachael Cartwright Lee had had enough. Dated 1860 through 1861, the pages recorded a divorce action with Rachael Lee as plaintiff and Job T. Lee as defendant. Even the handwriting seems troubled. My wife said she wasn't expecting this and turned the pages slowly as if to keep the air quiet. If anybody in Penny's family had known about this, no one ever said, embarrassed perhaps by such public revelations. Now on my desk lay the initial pleadings that constitute the petition for divorce. Page after page of testimony from family members and friends proclaim Rachael Lee "a kind & faithful wife," and Job Lee a sham as a husband. Another page is a "temporary order" that lists Job Lee's assets: two cows, one colt, thirteen hogs, two wagons, one yoke of cattle, and two-thirds interest in one hundred bushels of rye and sixty-five bushels of wheat, for a total value of $310. Another page requests that Rachael get custody of the minor children. Another asks for a restraining order, explaining that the plaintiff and the defendant have one son, Joseph, who is in the habit of getting intoxicated and is "utterly untrustworthy." At this moment, the defendant Job Lee is in jail for beating Rachael, and she is worried that Joseph would "squander and destroy the property as soon as the action for divorce is commenced."

❧   ❧   ❧

"This is painful," Penny said. "He's my family." Her first impulse was to shy away. I had never heard Rachael Cartwright Lee mentioned at a family gathering, and maybe the ruined garments of her domestic tragedy best lay folded and forgotten in a trunk in the attic. But the more I read, the easier it was to imagine a middle-aged woman my wife's height, with high cheekbones, perhaps graying hair tied up beneath a bonnet, her hands strong from cooking and cleaning and field work when necessary, dressed in a blue cotton day dress with a crocheted collar on the day she visits her lawyer's office in Spring Brook. He asked questions and she answered, hands in her lap. She knew her sons well, the ones she held close and the one she could not trust. She knew what Job owned, and what ought to be hers. And she knew that no cooked meal ready on time, no clean clothes, no waiting in a dark room, the candle pinched out, would change things now. Her lawyer, Mr. Bingham, might have asked her, was she sure?

"Penny," I said. "Look at this. After thirty years of marriage, your great-great-grandmother is standing up for herself. Has anyone told her story? None of what she did could have been easy."

Then a little research helped confirm the difficulties Rachael Lee faced by asking for a divorce in 1860. At fifty-five years old, she would have experienced the early nineteenth century's expectation of what a woman should be. In 1860, Rachael still had three children left at home, her "proper sphere." Historian Ellen Plante explains that women were expected to comfort their husbands, devote themselves to molding young children, and fashion "homes that were at once a retreat from the outside world and a material as well as a cultural inventory of refinement, social standing, intellect and honor. [The home] was the stage on which women played out their lives." As angel of the house, Rachael Lee served under the direction of social conventions, her husband, and her own history.

Rachael Lee's petition for divorce in Wisconsin wasn't futile, however, just difficult and audacious. Wisconsin became a state in 1848, and in 1849 adopted a Domestic Relations Code, which recognized six grounds for divorce: adultery, impotency, desertion for one year, imprisonment for three years, cruel and inhuman treatment, and habitual drunkenness. Although such a divorce law was considered liberal at the time, the prosecution of cases still proved difficult. My friend Len Sandler, who teaches at the University of Iowa's law school, showed me two early Wisconsin divorce cases, both presided over by the same magistrate, that set the conditions Rachael Lee must meet to prosecute her case successfully—an absolutely virtuous petitioner and the threat of severe bodily harm or death.

When Louisa Skinner's petition for divorce failed in 1856, the case turned on her husband, William, impugning her wanton behavior. She had filed for divorce on the grounds of his "cruel and inhuman treatment," which consisted of violence toward her, abusive language, and habitual drunkenness. William Skinner denied the allegations and testified that his wife, "frequently and repeatedly left *his* [italics mine] house and infant child to attend German balls and dances . . . that she has, against his consent, absented herself from home for weeks; that she has been in the habit of visiting brothels and houses of ill-fame, and of associating with notorious prostitutes and persons of lewd and infamous character." The presiding magistrate, Judge J. Cole, decided against her, arguing, "the petitioner has no right to complain. . . . She comes into a court of equity, asking to be divorced on the ground of ill-treatment received from her husband, when her own misconduct has undoubtedly brought upon her much, if not all, of the very treatment of which she complains." In other words, she asked for it and deserved everything she got.

Perhaps the more relevant—and dangerous—case for Rachael Lee was *Johnson v. Johnson*. Originally tried in circuit court in March of 1855, Mrs. Johnson's divorce was granted on the grounds that her husband's abusive language, his failure to provide, and his locking her out of the house were cruel and inhumane. However, in June of 1855, Mr. Johnson appealed to the Wisconsin Supreme Court, which overturned the verdict. Judge J. Cole stated that "Abusive and opprobrious language, which wounds the feelings merely, unaccompanied with bodily injuries, actual or menaced, is not considered a ground for divorce."

Historical studies of Wisconsin's legal system often cite *Johnson v. Johnson* as a defining case for what constitutes cruel and inhumane treatment, holding that cruelty was limited to conduct which "endangers the life and health of the wife, which exposes her to intolerable hardship and renders cohabitation unsafe." Len Sandler explained that *Johnson v. Johnson* also imposed stringent pleading and language requirements. Judge Cole decided that Mrs. Johnson's "allegation is too general and indefinite as it now stands, to support a charge of cruelty." If Rachael Lee wanted a divorce, she needed very specific language and concrete evidence to prove her life was in danger.

To that end, Rachael Lee found a good lawyer. In 1860, there were no women lawyers in Wisconsin; the first, Lavinia Goodell, started to practice in 1873. But in 1875, the Wisconsin Supreme Court denied her admission to the bar, stating, "The law of nature destines and qualifies the female sex for the bearing of children of our race and for the custody of the homes." Practicing law, the court went on to say, involves too much dirty business, there being so much "nastiness of the world" unfit for "female ears." Custodian of the house and "moulded for gentler and better things," Rachael Lee hired James Bingham to help clean up the painful business of her marriage.

First they had to establish her as a virtuous wife. By this time, Rachael had asked family members and friends to testify on her behalf: her brother, David Cartwright, Rachael's daughter, Martha Jane Fuller, and finally, a surprising witness, Hannah Lee, Rachael's mother-in-law and stepmother to Job Lee, who had lived with them for more than fifteen years. All vouched that the plaintiff had been "kind & faithful," each repeating those keys terms, with Hannah Lee adding that Rachael had performed more "faithfully & kindly than most women would under the circumstances."

Second, Mr. Bingham and Rachael defined the nature of Job Lee's "cruel and inhumane" treatment by providing dates and particular offenses, each numbered in a list of "items." Item VII, for example, reads, "That on the fifteenth day of December A.D. 1860 this defendant struck this plaintiff several heavy & violent blows on and about the head and face and kicked her and threw her over the stove with so much violence that it broke the stove and overturned various vessels on the stove & spilled scalding dye on her & he has threatened to kill her . . . . Her face became much swollen and very painful & made her unfit to perform her various household duties."

Depositions from family members verify these charges, mostly in heartbreaking terms. Two of the Lee sons, Phillip and Charles, spoke up, substituting the word "defendant" for "father" to keep a safe distance. Phillip said, "I have often known Defendant to come home drunk & abuse my mother by cuffing & striking her & pulling her hair, and kept her awake all night scolding & jawing & swearing at her & abusing her . . . . My mother was always kind to him & would sit up nights to keep supper ready for him when she expected him home."

Charles, who was sixteen at the time and still living at home, seconded Phillip, adding, "I saw the Defendant abuse my mother last December I think. He threw her on the bed & threw a quilt over her & soon after when my mother was taking a pan of biscuits out of the oven Defendant struck her on the side of the head & knocked her against the house."

Minerva Lee, a daughter-in-law, corroborates the broken stove incident. "On the night previous to this occasion, Defendant came home drunk & kept up a noisy quarrel with Plaintiff all night and in the morning my attention was particularly attracted by the noise of the stove as though something heavy had been thrown upon it and [heard] . . .

at the same time loud hollering and exclamations of pain & fright from Plaintiff." When Minerva went to look, she found Rachael "badly hurt & almost helpless on the floor." Job Lee told Rachael to stop crying, that she wasn't hurt, and he tried to make her stand up and finally sat her in a chair. Minerva said that "Plaintiff was covered with dye which was in a kettle upon the stove & the stove & vessels were overturned & scattered about the floor."

◌ ◌ ◌

Between the testimony's measured language and the chaos it alludes to, I imagine Rachael Lee shifting a pot onto the stove and then stirring in vegetable dye—indigo or the bark of red oak, boiled for days and then set with urine. Dye to finish his shirts or her cotton day dress. Indigo, the color of a bruise. Now the pots and pans lie helter-skelter. Spilled out, hot coals from the stove singe the floor's rough oak planking and soot drifts in a silent, ineffable cloud. One hundred and forty-eight years later, I hear her weeping. Standing in the middle of the kitchen, Job Lee tells her what she will do and what she isn't and what she doesn't feel, and she knows none of what he says is true. She knows the dye staining her hands and clothes will never wash out. She knows no needle and thread can mend such tearing. He lifts her by her arm to a chair. I imagine her bent over, head in her hands, having decided once and for all.

◌ ◌ ◌

Rachael Lee's lawyer, James Bingham, certainly knew that language such as "hair pulling," "cuffing," blows about the "head and face," and a face "blackened and swollen" could not be dismissed as "general and indefinite." But I think an even more convincing detail lies with the stove. Throughout the testimony it is obvious that Rachael Lee is in harm's way. Job Lee was physically and verbally abusive, but in 1860 that in itself may not have been reason enough to dissolve a marriage. What the broken stove and scattered vessels suggest is more ominous. Job Lee threatened the role of women in nineteenth-century culture. Their "sphere" was the home. Phillip Lee testified that his father threw his mother "against the house," against the symbol of all that women stood for and served. James Bingham was not about to argue against the notion of women as angels of the house, paragons of domesticity, keepers of the stove, servants to their husbands, and the nurturers of children. If anything, he was defending these cultural norms against assault by Job Lee.

Finally, the pleadings and depositions each describe Job Lee as a "habitual drunkard," a particularly damaging charge in 1860. An article by Catherine Cleary in the *Wisconsin Magazine of History* explains that by the middle 1850s, prohibition laws were on the Wisconsin legislative agendas and that the "liquor law" drew much attention during the 1855 legislative session. She writes, "The plight of women married to drunken husbands has become a focus of public attention nationally." Temperance societies had grown in popularity since the founding of the American Society for the Promotion of Temperance in Boston in 1826. In 1849, even the great showman P. T. Barnum produced a temperance melodrama titled *The Drunkard; or, The Fallen Saved*. He later traveled the country as a temperance speaker and wrote about the cause in his 1855 autobiography, *The Life of P. T. Barnum*, a book Samuel Clemens was said to admire.

By 1860, the lamentable and reviled "drunkard" must have seemed like a stock character universally despised, pitied, and subject to salvation by an evangelistic public. Job Lee's third youngest son, Phillip, testified, "My father the Defendant has been a drunkard ever since I can remember. Getting drunk every chance he could get. I have known him to be drunk for weeks at a time. He was in the habit of getting 4 or 5 gallons of whiskey & lying drunk while it lasted." Such prodigious drinking indeed, the equal fifteen years later to that of Huckleberry Finn's Pap, Twain's murderous reprobate, who thought his own four-gallon jug of whiskey enough "for two drunks and one delirium tremens."

◌ ◌ ◌

In the face of such overwhelming testimony and despite his lawyer, a Mr. W. T. Clothier, Job Lee finally withdrew his defense. On February 16, 1861, the Jefferson County circuit court judge H. S. Orton ordered that Rachael Lee be given sole "care custody services & education" of their three remaining minor children living at home—Phillip, Charles, and Harvey. The court also ordered that she be given an assortment of property such as cows and a horse, wheat and rye stores, and all the household furnishings in the "house of the Defendant and owned by him." Finally, Judge Orton declared the union dissolved and ordered "that it shall be lawful for the Plaintiff to marry again in the same manner as though the said Defendant was actually dead."

Incredibly, Rachael Lee had found language to do her husband in. In the middle of the nineteenth century, the only way a woman could be free of her husband was by means of his death, either literally or figuratively in the law. The principals in this story carried on with their lives, most prosperously. James Bingham fought as a major in the Union Army during the Civil War, went on to serve in the Wisconsin State Legislature, and was elected lieutenant governor in 1877. With her husband, Martha Jane Fuller set up and operated an important stagecoach stop called Half-way House outside of Spring Brook, Wisconsin. Charles remained close to his mother and helped her farm, and eventually purchased the farm from her. Phillip was shot and killed on June 11, 1864, at the Battle of Cold Harbor. Harvey, the youngest child, my wife's great-grandfather, farmed successfully in Eau Claire, Wisconsin, and married three times, even though a severe back injury confined him to a wheelchair.

Rachael Lee never married again. The 1870 United States census for the town of Spring Brook, lists Rachael Lee as sixty-five, not married, female, and white. She owns real estate valued at two thousand dollars and personal property valued at three hundred dollars, which made her one of the most affluent landowners in Spring Brook. Out of the thirty-five recorded farmers in that census district, Rachael Lee is the only woman and the only one whose occupation is listed as "farming" instead of "farmer." Perhaps the census taker in 1870 thought there was still a difference between what this woman did and who she should be—that is, the angel of the house. Her "proper sphere" was still the home. Conspicuous by his absence in the 1870 census is Job Lee, who left behind no further record after 1860. "Some say the wolves ate him," one reporter suggests, the sad metaphoric fate my mother-in-law relayed to me one hundred and fifteen years later. He's gone; even his death date is unknown.

"But think about this," I tell Penny. "We have rediscovered Rachael Cartwright Lee. Maybe this is where your dad got his persistence, all his endurance and toughness, all that resolve. It's from his great-grandmother. Even the Jefferson County Historical Society granted her the title 'true head of the family.'"

"Maybe," my wife says, growing silent, thinking, I'm sure, about what it took to survive in her own family—

when to retreat and when to stand up for herself. Perhaps I have made it all too simple, my in-laws and wife a complex mix of motives and emotions. But I do know that she grew up in a family in which the wolf wandered generation after generation, that she has stood up to being bullied, that she confronted her mother's alcoholism. When we decided at last to move across the country for school and work, I remember her telling me how her father came unglued. Red-faced, fist in hand, he marched toward her, insisting that she stay for the sake of her mother, that no daughter of his would leave him like this.

"But I am your daughter," Penny would have said, firmly, "and I have my own family now and we're going to move." What she wouldn't have explained is that her opportunities lay elsewhere and she knew it. Couched in four generations of resolve, her answer did not sit well with her father. But sit it did.

My wife is the great-great-granddaughter of Rachael Cartwright Lee, a daughter of the American Revolution, we suspect, who stood up to domestic tyranny and saved her "good name" to pass along to the future. This Penny and I can verify. We stand up and speak for her now.

Posting

In my assigned corner, I sat in a 1950s chrome and vinyl armchair and waited for my daughter, Meryl, to finish her riding lesson in the Diamond W Stables indoor arena. The smell of hay and sweat thickened the air. At my feet, sparrows scavenged horsehair to build nests in the rafters. Through broken roof shingles, sunlight spotlighted Meryl posting up and down on Tosca, a small saddle mare—butt on top of butt. Tosca seemed calm and far less tragic than her namesake. Outside, a farrier's hammer rang out. Meryl was eleven. Her black helmet and blue fleece bobbing away from me in a swirl of dust.

That was thirteen years ago. Just last week, my friend Marvin called and asked if we still had the riding helmet that he and his wife, Dorothy, had passed along to us when they learned our daughter wanted to ride. I thought it might still be in the basement. In boxes and bags, I found much she has left behind: CDs, photos, albums, cross-country ski boots. She was here in artifact but not in person, now that she had grown up and moved away. I rummaged, our basement tidier than my memory.

How easy it is to get sidetracked. There were ballet slippers, and a few dolls for which she had sewn dresses—tiny felt skirts with big stitches. Beneath catalogues for horse gear and riding clothes, there were drawings in notebooks, page after of page of slender girls and simple dresses, as if Meryl were designing a concept of herself. Then as she grew into her teens, the compositions turned darker, collages of torn paper and photos touched up or disrupted, 35mm film negatives tipped in. In one, she stares at herself in a mirror, her black hair—white in the negative—cut short and severe. There are pronouncements and rhetorical questions scribbled over the top of drawings, almost a palimpsest of wonder and frustration framed by staccato punctuation marks. A few pages lie ink-washed nearly to black, as if a Midwest storm had rolled in, thunder and rain and hail imminent. The weather just seemed out of control.

Even now this testimony hurts. Sometimes I could only stand there, saying things are OK, knowing they weren't, and no, that I probably didn't understand, but I'd be here or downstairs or waiting in a corner if you need me. Afraid for her, I wondered what I might have done to contribute to her struggles.

There are cards and notes to her mother and me and drawings we keep. Here's one where she celebrates my birthday. She made the card herself, applying the coolest descriptors in her vocabulary. She was in the third grade. The only hitch in the composition was that she still reversed letters and spelled creatively. Thus, when I opened my birthday card, I was greeted with "For Dab, a cool rab boob, love, Meryl." True on both counts, I believe, noble fathers relegated to the corner of a stable to be seen and not heard. But anxious and watching nonetheless.

One of Meryl's teachers said that she wasn't too concerned when her students reverse letters. "It's like mixing up the east wall in the classroom with the west," she explained. "It's when someone confuses the floor with the ceiling that we get concerned."

I understood, having gotten lost myself. Early in school, I had trouble ordering my world, as taken as I was with daydreaming. My grade school window opened onto the wind and the pine-soaked woods of Hamlin Park in Seattle, while behind me the paraphernalia of numbers and sequence and order cluttered up my desk, filled its drawer and lay scattered in books about my feet, enough so that the janitors complained. My mother showed me the notes.

I'm sorry. Maybe I visited my sins upon Meryl, for she too imagined well but struggled to order and sequence and balance herself in the world. How instructions faded a moment after they were given. How names simply disappeared. School became painful. Nothing lined up in a row. *Oh, how I understand, sweetheart.* And even though Meryl was smart and brave enough to ask her teachers in grade school to repeat instructions so she could write them down (an exercise recommended by learning psychologists, incidentally, to help students process information), a few teachers scolded her, complaining that she wasn't paying attention or that she daydreamed excessively.

"She's trying to fix this herself," I said, angry with myself as much as her teachers.

"Yes, I know," my wife said, and I thought of Auden's line, "And our teachers report that [she] never interfered with their education."

Determined, Penny searched until she found teachers who understood how Meryl learned and were happy to help. Sitting in my dusty corner, I was glad Penny and Meryl had also found Diamond W Stables, where this eleven-year-old girl could set about finding east and west in her own body. Tosca was her mount and compass.

Fascinated by riding catalogues, Meryl had signed up for riding lessons, ostensibly beginning dressage, sometimes called "horse ballet." Even the names for simple movements in dressage suggest ballet: "passage" for slow-motion trot, "piaffe" for trotting in place, and "pirouettes" for 360-degree circles in place. At its most advanced, dressage involves movements such as "capriole" or "courbette," where the horse leaps off the ground or performs a series of hops on its back legs.

◇   ◇   ◇

Meryl's riding addressed more basic issues. By the grimace on her face, I could see how hard she had to work to keep Tosca on a straight line toward me—thinking through her hands and hips into the reins and saddle and out through the horse and into the direction she was moving. She worked hard at finding her seat, a kind of grammar of the body, what stays parallel, what lies subordinate, what remains independent. How the body balances in space, up and down, right and left, stopping and starting. And in the middle of all this, how to center the swirl of her own mind, thoughts given voice through knees and hands easy beneath the reins, which tied her to the soft mouth of Tosca. Then Tosca trotted by and turned away, Meryl's head straight, arms relaxed and back straight, her legs bent at the knees as she stood in the stirrups, posting.

Even simpler yet, Meryl's riding allowed her contact with an animal larger than herself that needed tending and care, that required her to listen and relax and pay attention, to give in and lead at the same time. The poet and horse-woman Maxine Kumin explains in her essay "Silver Snaf-fles," that "the horse often comes into a young girl's life at a time when she feels the need to take control of some measure of what is essentially an uncontrollable environ-ment. . . . When all else shifts, changes and disappoints, the horse can remain constant." It is a wish for fathers as well.

◇   ◇   ◇

Though not by disposition Jane Smiley's "horsy girl," Meryl knew that if she wanted to ride, she needed to shovel horse manure and muck out the stables and clean the tack and name its parts. She needed to saddle the horse and fit the bridle and tighten the straps and climb on. At the end of her ride, she needed to dismount and lead the horse into the stable, secure it with ties at both sides of the bridle so she might unstrap the saddle, and wipe Tosca down and brush her and lift her legs below the knee and clean her hooves with a pick. Next to an eleven-year-old, Tosca was huge—nine hundred pounds of warm muscle and rib cage.

I'm thinking of a lovely moment when Meryl brushed Tosca out after one ride, left hand on her withers, right hand brushing down her spine over and over. And then Meryl leaned her left ear against Tosca's side as if listening to her heart, and the look on Meryl's face suggested music, a tune she hummed to herself all the car ride home, looking out the window, the smell of horse in her hair and clothes.

Through this process, these steps, this work, Meryl had to pay attention and be respectful, for Tosca was an animal at every moment worthy of fear. The problem might be as simple as Tosca stepping on her foot. Or worse. I remember two of Meryl's riding friends brushing Pearl, another stable mare that stood day after day docile in her tethers. Except this one day. Maybe it was a bee or a horsefly. Impossible to say over Pearl's screaming and wild bucking as two girls, their helmets askew and riding jackets unzipped, scrambled over the side of the stall and knelt down behind the wood fence, wide-eyed, almost in reverence, to watch their sweet mare splinter the wall behind with steel shoes.

All of them rode the next day. They followed the steps needed and tended the animals and rode, these girls. From my corner, I could only guess what was going on inside them, except to say they had found a wonderful and fearful analogue for their ride on the journey to womanhood. I was anxious for Meryl and told her, and she said, "Oh, Dad."

Thinking back, I'm not sure if I was worried more about Meryl's falling off or whether she would fit in. It was clear from my corner that Diamond W Stables was a woman's domain. Martha, the owner, conducted business from an office filled with horse pictures and ribbons and a century's worth of tack. Even the couch was covered by a saddle blanket. Her favorite horse was Pete, a white stallion, seventeen hands tall and muscle bound. "He gets away from me," she said once when I asked about him, "and I just hang on." Martha hired the grooms and trainers, all young women, the hierarchy in Diamond W plain, from beginning riders up to the stable vet, Sylvia, sitting to my left now on a two-year-old, high-stepping, and excitable quarter horse.

From what I could overhear, the woman standing next to Martha had flown up from California to consider this quarter horse for purchase. Another woman, maybe the horse's owner, her arms folded, stood next to them but looked down at the dirt floor of the arena and scraped it with her toe, as if to underscore what she was hearing. Talking, nodding, all three of them stood in a knot before the beautiful, athletic bay and touched him and laughed as the vet reined the horse one way, then another.

On the far side of the arena through the dust haze, I saw Meryl and Tosca, one two one two in their methodical posting through the alphabet around the perimeter of the arena. My first memory of her that morning was her riding away from me, ponytail swinging behind her blue fleece. As I think back over the years, this riding away is not an uncommon image. A few minutes after Meryl was born, the nurse handed her to me and she began to cry. Her mother, who'd had a hard labor, said in a tired voice from her bed, "Oh, don't cry." Incredibly, Meryl stopped, opened her eyes and turned back toward the voice, a voice she knew. Already she was on her way to find out who she was and what was out there and maybe even what she had left behind. Each time she rode away—to visit friends, to camp, to school, to Baltimore and Goucher College, and to a future she had sketched out for us in the vaguest terms—I watched her go. When she turned back to look, as she always did, her face skeptical and squinting at my concern, I waved.

That morning on Tosca, Meryl turned at the far end of the arena and trotted toward the preoccupied ensemble of horse and horsewomen. I worried that they expected Meryl to take the initiative, breaking her rhythmic pattern and swinging wide enough to miss them. After all, in contrast to their lively negotiations, Meryl's riding seemed perfunctory, a simple drill. Not the ride of the acrobatic girl, certainly, in E. B. White's "The Ring of Time," who "swung herself off and on the horse several times," who most of the time "simply rode in a standing position, well aft of the beast, her hands hanging easily at her sides." Nor the daring of the sixteen-year-old, whom a friend of mine hired to exercise his expensive, racing quarter horse, who rode shoeless and bareback as the horse ran and ran in circles. She rode effortlessly, her hair flying in the wind like an extension of the yellow mane she held onto with both hands.

No, Meryl and Tosca plodded on in good form, learning sequence and rules, the boring stuff Meryl would say later, reins held lightly, Tosca chewing. I didn't know what was going to happen, until the women simply stopped what they were doing. The owner and the buyer and Martha edged back against the side of the arena and grew quiet. The vet lifted up on her reins and the lovely, spirited bay bounced a few steps back toward the center of the arena, and through the middle of them all, between the parting sea of negotiation and ownership and community of horsewomen, Meryl and Tosca posted up and down as regular and balanced as a heartbeat.

Meryl didn't seem surprised, and maybe I shouldn't have been either. Maybe they all started with such a horse on a similar line, and these women were simply honoring nostalgia. Maybe they wanted to size up a new rider, to watch her form. But looking back, I can't help but see this moment as significant. A girl alone on her easy mount, exercising her body and mind, Meryl circled the far edge of the arena before she turned and passed through a congregation of women who loved horses, who by their silence and deference and parting ushered Meryl into their company. Meryl was on a circular journey, and from where I stood, someone young rode away, and someone new, older, more self-sufficient rode back, and waved, and then went by. I was happy for her.

To keep the record clear, I was not ignored entirely at Diamond W Stables. I got my short ride. One day, Martha said I should ride Venture, just to get a feel for it, just to give it a try.

"No, I'm not a rider," I said. "Happy to watch."

"Here. Take him an apple," she said. "He's in stall ten. Keep your palm flat."

Venture was huge, eighteen hands, a black-coated thoroughbred saved by Martha. Some years back, he'd had a run-in with a barbed wire fence and had badly torn up his right front leg. After an infection set in, he was so sick that his owners decided to put him down. But Martha cleared a space in the middle of the arena and nursed Venture over the winter, and little by little he regained his strength with only a permanently stiff right front leg to show for his ordeal. Martha had two thoroughbreds after that, the white with blinding speed and the black that hobbled along. She was afraid to ride one and wouldn't ride the other, but kept both because she loved them.

"What do you think? Should I try?" I asked Meryl.

"Why not," she said.

Eighteen hands means my seat was six feet in the air. I needed a stool just to get my left foot in the stirrup and grunted and lifted to swing my right leg up and over, and then I was straddling a very broad back. I'm sure the sparrows panicked. Martha held Venture on one side of his bridle, looked up at me in the dusty air, aimed the horse down the middle of the arena, and let go. Before I knew it, Venture had vaulted on three good legs and one bad to the far end of the arena. My head missed the rafters. I remember the ride hurt, especially where my hips and legs join and at the base of my spine and everywhere in between. Signaling to get off, please, I looked back at Meryl who stood beside Martha, laughing behind her hand, her dad a "cool rab boob" at last.

◊　◊　◊

I never found the riding helmet. Penny said that Meryl had decided to stop riding because she had learned what she needed. When I asked Meryl what she most enjoyed about Diamond W Stables, she said galloping, and then jumping when Martha finally allowed it. But even that wasn't enough to hold Meryl on Tosca, and by the time she started high school, she was on to other journeys. Penny said that we had passed the helmet on to Hannah down the street who rode until she found herself and then passed the helmet to Jennifer who passed it to Amber and so on in a circle. I called Marvin to say that I was sorry, that we had passed the helmet on to another girl, and he said yes, that's what it was for.

So Much More

Correspondence

I had not heard from my cousin Jean for years, so when I first saw her letter, the return address San Francisco, I was overjoyed. Maybe she had read my new book, which contained an essay about her mom, who swam in the 1936 Olympics. I was pleased with the essay, thought it was a loving tribute to my aunt, our family's first athlete. Maybe Jean was pleased as well. But I was wrong about that.

The essay had many sources: our family's obvious pride in having such an athlete in our midst, the eccentricity and story potential of her participating in the Nazi Olympics in Berlin, my seeing for the first time Leni Riefenstahl's *Olympia*, and finally, my ongoing ambivalence whenever I teach A. E. Housman's poem, "To an Athlete Dying Young." Well and good, I once thought, if an athlete dies before his fame runs out, a fitting and perhaps romantic conclusion, my being young and in the best shape of my life. But the older I get, the more the death-before-anonymity option seems premature. Did Housman really believe that, or did he fashion such a sentiment to ease a moment of grief? The poem makes me wonder just what happens to an athlete who does grow old. I'm growing older.

I thought I might find an answer when I discovered *Olympia* and the brief appearance of my aunt, Olive McKean, in the final of the women's 100-meter freestyle event, three hours into the documentary and in the middle of part two. She was twenty-one and placed sixth. When I called my aunt sixty-one years later, she said she had never seen the film. "Might I visit?" I asked, and hearing a confirmation, I started to work and study so I might ask worthwhile questions, for I had no idea what she might remember or how she might react to my prompts.

She remembered everything, lap for lap, especially about her bronze medal finish in the 4 x 100 relay and then her effort in the 100-meter individual event. *Olympia* named each swimmer in the women's 100-meter freestyle, Olive McKean assigned to lane three. When the gun discharged, she sat on the edge of her chair and urged herself down to the turn and then into the home stretch and sat back after her one-minute-eight-second finish, disappointed and exhausted even by the memory. "Too high, too high," she said, critiquing her position in the water. For years, she had been the coach for the Multnomah Swim Club in Portland, Oregon, and as I watched her watching herself, she adopted her coaching demeanor, jaw clenched, brow furrowed, critical, analyzing her technique—how she got off the block late, how she lurched at the end of the race, fatigue having set in. And then she said, "I wish I had worked harder. I swam the best time of my life."

How appropriate—the athlete's dilemma of dissatisfaction. You've done fine but there's always something better, the urge to win, the need to outdo your opponent, most often yourself, always pushing. She was eighty-two, and the urgency was still there. The race was still there, the memory timeless. Her revelation felt intimate and like a gift to me. In my essay, I tried to explain how such transcendent moments belie time. Housman's "glory" may not have stayed, but in my aunt's face I saw how one brief moment had survived. Fascinated and encouraged by her conflating time, I had written, "[T]he 100-meter freestyle was her philosophical source, a lens through which she focused sixty-one years of turbulent history." Fifty meters, a turn, and fifty meters more in a single lane stood as a metaphor for an athlete's need to focus and thus remember. A minute and eight seconds, played again and again, with the same outcome. A life centered. A way to grow old and stay young.

For this my cousin's letter, in one short, typed paragraph, charged me with betrayal. How could I write such things? "I still feel very disappointed with your willingness to hurt Mom. The woman you portrayed as so strong was brought to tears by your betrayal." Why hadn't I let either her (Jean) or Judy, her younger sister, review the manuscript? I was baffled. What had I said? That my aunt had enjoyed the novelty of seeing Hitler poolside and then late one afternoon at a rally somewhere in Berlin? That my aunt had missed the bus back to the Olympic quarters after a party held by Joseph Goebbels, drinking champagne and flirting with a German soldier? No, Olive seemed pleased when she told me those stories. What then? My focus on that one race? "How Mom cried and cried," Jean mentioned, "that she was so much more, so much more."

I folded the letter back into its envelope and tried to think of what I'd missed. After all, my cousin Judy, Jean's younger sister, had seen drafts of the essay and offered helpful edits and comments in the margins. Happy to recount her trip to Berlin, my aunt hadn't volunteered, however, a word about her career after her experience at the Olympics. And alas, I hadn't thought to ask.

The fact is, my aunt never commented on my essay, at least not to me. Her next Christmas card read as politely and warmly as her cards always had. Faced with a visit from my aunt and her daughters the summer after my book was published, my mother read the essay again to prepare. "You don't have to defend me," I told her on the phone, to which she replied, "I don't know what Olive's complaining about." They visited my mother for three days and no one raised the subject.

Then my aunt died on March 31, 2006, almost a year later. She was ninety-one, but it was too soon. I regret not addressing the issue with her, though I'm still not sure exactly what the issue was. Our family avoids such conflicts, retreating to the far corners of the continent and polite silence. Who was talking or not talking, and to whom? What did my aunt's lament mean? "I was so much more." True, she was a great coach, and tough and sympathetic enough to drive her charges to Olympic-caliber levels, serving as manager and chaperone for the women's swim team in two Olympics, first in Mexico City in 1968, and then in Munich in 1972. She was the first woman president in the history of the Oregon Amateur Athletic Union. She was elected to swimming hall of fame after swimming hall of fame, and spent twenty years coaching at the Multnomah Athletic Club.

These are remarkable achievements and certainly "much more" than I had addressed. But such credentials don't reveal her story, the struggles she went through as an athlete in the face of world-class competition. How did she manage that solitary grind to success? It's heady at the end but hurts to get there. Who was she? I didn't know where to turn until my cousin Judy offered a surprise. Her mother had kept meticulous scrapbooks and had donated them long ago to the International Swimming Hall of Fame in Fort Lauderdale, Florida, without informing anybody in the family. When Judy found out, she became upset and asked why she had never seen them. Aunt Olive said only that she didn't think Judy would be interested.

I was interested in these scrapbooks. Housman laments "runners who renown outran / And the name died before the man." Maybe Olive wanted to fix her name for posterity, to note her accomplishments without celebration, to slow the race, or maybe even disqualify "renown" as an adversary. In the silence, I had another chance to visit my aunt.

Fort Lauderdale

My aunt's scrapbooks sat in a cardboard box on a shelf in a back closet of the library of the International Swimming Hall of Fame behind an ornate album celebrating Buster Crabbe. They were not catalogued, and to find them we had to know what to ask for. I called the Hall of Fame curator several times, verified the scrapbooks' existence, and made an appointment to visit. When I finally opened the box, five years of Olive's swimming life lay bound on a reading table. Comprised mostly of newspaper clippings interspersed with swim meet announcements and programs and rosters, the scrapbooks stack eight inches high. After seventy years, the clippings were fragile. Newsprint is not destined to last, a fate assigned, as Housman speculated, to all our athletic achievements.

The first entry is dated in August 1930, the last in July of 1935, a year before her participation in the 1936 Olympics. And when I thumbed through her first careful pages, each small clipping taped in and meticulously recorded with a date and newspaper source, I was suddenly overwhelmed by how close I felt to what she had hidden away. She looks like me when I was lost and awkward at fourteen, mouth open and wide-eyed and searching the camera for any affirmation. She's nearly six feet tall, a sophomore at Ballard High School in Seattle. She swims in Seattle's Green

Lake all summer while her mother works. In a *Seattle Times* photo, she stands in her swimsuit and cap, her right arm around the waist of a teammate, and her left hand reaching for a medal. The caption reads "Rewarding Champions: Mrs. H. F. Alexander presents the medal to the winning relay team, Frieda Alder, Pat Linden, Jacquelyn Garton, and Olive McKean." Mrs. Alexander, a prominent Seattle socialite sporting a fashionable scarf and white cloche hat, hands my aunt the medal, who studies it as if it predicts her future, the brass and ribbons verifying and locating her in the history of Green Lake swimming competitions. My aunt already has two medals pinned to her swimsuit, perhaps for winning earlier races that day. She stands a head taller than Mrs. Alexander and the rest of the swimmers. My aunt has written August 1930 and *Seattle Times* next to the clipping. She has just turned fifteen.

Her mother, my grandmother, works as a seamstress. Her father, my grandfather, tends a cigar store in downtown Seattle. Olive's older brother, my father, rides the trains to eastern Washington to harvest wheat, working behind mule-driven combines. By 1934 my father would enlist in the Army and be stationed in Hawaii. Their younger brother, my uncle Don, keeps to himself in their basement, mysterious and unknown, I can only imagine, before his stint in reform school. The market crashed in 1929 and the Depression was reason enough for my father to drop out of high school and look for work. Given the hard times and my grandfather's disability—a leg lost in a mill accident—and his drinking, and given what I know about my grandmother—herself the survivor of foster care and the logging towns of southwest Washington—I suspect there was little room for a dreamer in this home.

What expectations did a teenage girl have for herself in 1930? My aunt is tall and strong, the middle child, a girl between two brothers, who enjoys Saturday movie matinees and listening to the radio at night. Maybe she reads Dashiell Hammett or Pearl S. Buck. Maybe she vamps behind her bedroom door like Greta Garbo or Jean Harlow. And when she isn't chatting with her friends from Ballard High, she swims as often as she can at West Green Lake Beach. In *Their Day in the Sun: Women of the 1932 Olympics*, Doris Pieroth explains how "the [Seattle] Park Department ran an extensive beach swimming program" at Green Lake, "with University of Washington students as teachers, coaches, and lifeguards." They undoubtedly encouraged Olive McKean in one of the sports acceptable for women in the 1920s and '30s. Pieroth notes that after World War I, "the sportswoman became an ubiquitous symbol in advertising wars to promote and sell a wide range of products. This embrace of free enterprise allowed women 'to become not merely athletic but athletes—*as long as they understood their femininity with the right sports and attire.*'" I'm not sure what my aunt may have understood about her femininity, but I do know she had been singled out for her swimming, and her size and potential. I remember how such positive reinforcement felt and what it did for my self-concept as I played basketball. A line in a sidebar about the winning basket, or a word or two about what I'd just done and what I might accomplish in the future. Like my aunt at that nexus moment, medal in hand, I found myself fleetingly happy.

Then someone discovered her. Until I opened those first scrapbooks, I'd never thought of my aunt as a dreamer, nor as a shy teenager. But here on the first page of the first scrapbook, above a man's picture, she has hand-printed in caps "SWIMMING" and below that "BOOK 1." In the lower right corner of the page she has printed "OLIVE MCKEAN." Unnamed, the man sits in his coat and tie in the middle of her title page, centered in a story she composes for herself. His name is Ray Daughters. His presence runs all through these scrapbooks and their coach-athlete relationship inevitably grows more complicated and intense as the years go by. But now there seems to be a girlish blush in the careful trimming and centering of his picture, his name kept to herself.

Ray Daughters, a former West Coast swimming champion and swim coach for Seattle's Crystal Natatorium since 1924, had already pushed Helene Madison, a senior at Seattle's Lincoln High School, to remarkable times in local swim meets. By March of 1930, she had gained national fame by setting a world record of 1:40.2 in the 150-yard freestyle. David Eskenazai writes that Ray Daughters "first spotted Madison as a gangly 14-year-old in the summer of 1927, taking part in the *Post Intelligencer*'s annual Swim Carnival at Green Lake." Lacking technique, Helene "had done nothing to distinguish herself from other girls her age . . . [b]ut Daughters focused on her height—5' 11"—big bones and the way she naturally navigated the water."

My aunt was such a girl—five feet eleven—and powerful at fifteen. With his "practiced eye" Ray Daughters may have spotted her at Green Lake in 1930. It makes sense. Aided and abetted by circumstances and fortune and this persistently ambitious man, who recognized raw talent, who balanced praise with comparisons, flattery with expectations, my aunt surely believed his narrative of what she might accomplish, of who she might be. Handsome, middle-aged but younger than her father, this man paid attention to her and articulated a dream she had yet to imagine for herself. Not only that, Daughters must have convinced her mother that the time and effort necessary to swim competitively were worthwhile. The membership fees at the new Washington Athletic Club, a cost her family could not afford, would be covered because her daughter had talent and the right attitude. After all, the 1932 Olympics were only two years away, and Olive must give her full attention to preparing. It must have been heady stuff.

I have had such coaches myself, who align your promise with theirs. The pain isn't mentioned. That's to come, after your mentor lays a hand on your shoulder and wakes you into motion.

* * *

Now another image comes to mind. My aunt sits on the side of the Washington Athletic Club swimming pool, her feet distorted beneath the surface, and searches the light reflecting off the water. Pumps hum beneath the floor. She has taken the trolley downtown, perhaps riding with her father to his corner cigar shop and then walking the six blocks back up the hill to the club, quiet this early Wednesday morning in summer. She's by herself. It's her birthday, August 10, 1932. Seventeen, she plans to celebrate later that evening after her mother and father finish work.

Right now she's alone and feeling foolish perhaps and certainly down, for she has been left behind. The newspapers in the rack next to her father's till this morning announce Helene Madison's Olympic gold medal, won two days earlier in the 100-meter freestyle. Helene, the star of the Washington Athletic Club and darling of the Seattle swimming scene, and my aunt's teammate, will swim in the 4 x 100 three days from now, one thousand miles away in Los Angeles. My aunt kicks her feet in the water. Hadn't she been celebrated as having Olympic-caliber promise? Hadn't she worked hard these last two years? Was she simply naïve? The light off the water won't answer. All she can hear is the pump circulating the water in the WAC pool— the chlorine smell everywhere—and the echo of locker room doors.

When Olive dives into the lane, it's to swim hard until the burning in her muscles mutes the disappointment in her heart. It's to help her forget what her mentor had told the *Seattle Times*: "I expect to prepare Miss McKean for the 400-meter event of the Olympics and it is my opinion that she will be one of the outstanding stars of that 1932 meet." His opinion was then repeated, as near as her high school newspaper and as far away as the *New York Times*. Maybe such burning helps her realize that being "Smiling Olive," and "one of the fastest developing youngsters in these parts," means little if her times are slow. Her friends at the Ballard High School newspaper say she's "young, bashful and modest and cheerful" on one hand and "a lithe graceful water shark" on the other. She's a "regular girl, a swell friend," they say, such demeanor acceptable for a teenage girl in 1932. Where does that get you? my aunt might ask herself, touching the edge of the pool and turning to push off into one more lap in two hours' worth of laps. Back and forth. Her breathing labors and her shoulders go numb. But these aren't reasons enough to stop. Something's driving her now, something shark-like.

I remember the motivations to work hard in athletics— ambition, anger, fear, frustration, spite, embarrassment, envy, even the need to please a coach, the one person who convinces you the pain you suffer is worthwhile. My aunt must have suffered but did so in silence, I'm sure, lap after lap, debating at each turn about her potential as a swimmer and the fact of being abandoned. I tried to find out why she'd been left behind, but there are only a few clippings for those months prior to the August 1932 Olympics and none that say why she wasn't chosen. One piece in the *Seattle Star* dated May 1, 1932, welcomes the WAC swimming team home from the national A.A.U. indoor championship at Los Angeles where my aunt swam in the winning 400-meter relay team. "National indoor events and the Olympics are yet to come. In each of these you'll hear of these young ladies and always you'll find Seattle's name, the Washington Athletic Club's name, carried after them." A

Seattle P.I. article dated May 11, 1932, celebrates the team's accomplishments in Los Angeles and adds, "Olive McKean, the 'Personality Kid' of the team, made a big hit with the critics down South, and all the railbirds were unanimous in handing her 'the duke' as a coming star." When I looked up the participants in the 1932 Olympics swimming tryouts held July 15 and 16 at Jones Beach, Long Island, New York, I found Helene Madison and Edna McKibben from the WAC. But not Olive McKean.

Birthdays tend to complicate one's mood. Tired after her two-hour workout, she waits for the trolley home. Perhaps this is her testing moment when she no longer focuses on what the price is for chasing her dreams, when she realizes that charm and deference—always upbeat, smiling—all the ephemera of popularity and promise, all the expectations of being a woman athlete in the right sport, are beside the point now that the universe has called her out to say you're not good enough. Even though it's close to noon in August in Seattle, my aunt pulls a sweater around her as if she's just felt a chill. Her skin is dry, her short hair combed back and still damp. Not good enough, she admits. Not yet.

The headline in the *Seattle Times* sports section dated August 23, 1932, speaks to Olive McKean's commitment to a journey she has made for herself. "Coach Returns to Discover He Has a New Star." Something happened to my aunt while the WAC swim club competed in Los Angeles. Regret? Anger? Or the simple realization of what she must do for herself and by herself if she is to succeed? "Upon his return to Seattle from the Olympic Games Daughters found Miss McKean had been training daily in the club pool, while the Winged W team was away, and was ready to show him speed over her favorite distance—220 yards." "To show him" is the operative phrase. The article continues, "Coming back to Seattle after her mates went east, the young mermaid decided to waste no time perfecting herself in the stroke and form that Daughters had taught her. Thus after two months of hard training, she was all set and ready to show her speed to Daughters in an early trial upon his return."

Show him she did. Alone in the WAC pool, with Daughters standing at the edge holding a stopwatch, my aunt swam the 220 in 2 minutes 34.8 seconds, nearly six seconds faster than Helene Madison's time at that distance three years earlier in a similar cold trial. This is what I imagine about my aunt: she was willing to commit, to struggle, to train exhaustively despite her fear of failure or family hardship. As smiling and popular as she may have been, celebrated by the newspaper and her high school chums, she slipped alone into the WAC pool day after day to ask herself what she truly wanted and what it would take, and what to do with her old deferential self, the one willing to please, who would do anything for her coach. With each lap she left that girl farther behind and pulled herself out at the end of her workout gasping to a new self, one with an edge.

She experienced less anger, I imagine, than determination, less a set of lofty coach-articulated ideals than her own exercise in grit. Even when the newspaper runs her picture with the caption saying "Personality Plus—That's Olive McKean, one of the sweetest kids that ever donned a bathing suit. When Olive isn't pulling herself through the water she always wears a big smile." From a distance, a smile and grimace can look the same. I imagine her focused on what it takes to "pull herself through the water." That's the only point, as she works hard to perfect her coach's "Japanese Double Arm pull," a freestyle stroke that delivers more power especially combined with a "highly perfected and powerful leg stroke." She can smile later. She will make that freestyle stroke and leg kick her own. She will not be left behind. The 1936 Olympics is four years away.

By this time in her scrapbooks, I notice Ray Daughters' picture no longer graces the title pages.

Ninth and Pine

From 1933 to 1936, Olive's scrapbooks are less formal compositions and more a place to store her impressive news, for my aunt has begun to set records on her own, to make a name for herself, first as another Helene Madison and then simply as herself. Programs for national swim meets in Chicago and Detroit, plus all the requisite newspaper clippings, celebrate her performance in individual events as well as a member of the WAC's 400-meter relay team. On October 6, 1933, the *Caldwell News Tribune* featured a picture of my aunt swimming the crawl beneath the headline "Splashing to a New World Record." The caption explains, "Olive McKean of the Washington Athletic Club, paddles her way to a new record in the 400-meter swim for women during the Far Western A.A.U. swimming and diving championships recently held in Los Angeles." Looking back through her scrapbooks, I find that at one time or another she held a world record in the 220-yard freestyle and the American record in the 250-yard and the 500-yard freestyle events. By February 15, 1935, the WAC's women's 400-yard relay team, for which she was the anchor, had broken their own world mark with a 4:13.3/5 for the indoor short pool. Then they set the long course world record at the April 1935 A.A.U. National Senior Swimming and Diving Championships in Chicago with a time of 4:15.3. In the April 1934 National Indoor Championships in Chicago, Olive McKean won the 100-meter indoor freestyle championship, defeating the reigning champ Lenore Kight. In July of that year at the outdoor championships in Detroit, my aunt won again to hold both 100-meter freestyle national titles at once. She repeated in 1935, as did the relay team in 1936. The finale, of course, was her qualifying for the Olympic team in July of 1936 and competing that August in Berlin.

◊　◊　◊

These are the facts. Reviewing this amazing record, I wonder if this is what she meant by being so much more. I wonder if anyone besides another athlete realizes what kind of work ethic she must have had. A January 29, 1935, *Seattle P.I.* column "The Morning After," written by Seattle's famous journalist Royal Brougham, states that "Being a Champion is Not Fun at All" and "Look at the Schedule of Miss McKean." Calling my aunt a leading candidate for Olympic Game honors, the column outlines her regimen: no candy, no pie à la mode or cigarettes. Then two hours of strenuous training every day in the WAC pool, driven relentlessly by Ray Daughters, who asks her first to do thirty laps using the hand board so just her legs and feet do the work.

Then it's chasing "Little Charlie," a Ray Daughters–controlled invention, consisting of a flag on a string attached to a machine. Switched into motion, the flag sets a pace, something akin to the mechanical rabbit in a dog race. Then as the date for the meet draws closer, her training is all sprint work. Ten, twenty times in a row, responding to the starter's gun, then drive, drive, drive down the lane, turn and drive back. Brougham's list is exhausting to read until he quotes my aunt, "'But don't get the idea that it's all monotonous work,' the champion explained the other day, as she balanced her slim powerful body on the spring board. 'We have lots and lots of fun while we are training.'" Fun? That sounds like her. I can hear her once again on those Christmas vacations when she and my uncle watched me play basketball in Portland's Far West

Classic, my body so sore and exhausted afterward that I always wondered what she meant by saying, "I hope you had fun." Well, fun now that it's over, I thought, and even more fun when the aching stops.

I don't believe it was fun that drove my aunt through those grueling workouts. "Ray Daughters kept the club's swimmers constantly in the news," Pieroth writes, "busy in the pool, operating on a shoestring. They swam endless workouts, promotional exhibitions, local meets . . . [and] gave frequent exhibitions for the entertainment of club members." Obviously delighted at being a member of the WAC swim team, my aunt explained to Doris Pieroth that "I felt very fortunate to be selected . . . I just remember that I was very much awed to come into that [the Washington Athletic Club's] beautiful locker room . . . and having a locker all your own. It was very impressive to someone who really . . . was naïve as I was at the time." Even today she sounds very young, a girl in the middle of the Depression who had never imagined such a facility, or such privilege. What a luxury to have her own locker, and if she had to work herself to exhaustion to keep it, then so be it. Doris Pieroth explains that neither the young women on the WAC swim team nor their families could afford to belong to the Washington Athletic Club. "The girls often wore hand-me-down clothing. More than one recalled, 'We were all poor—we had nothing.'"

Then Doris Pieroth solved a puzzle for me. Tucked in with the 1934 newspaper clippings, I found Olive McKean's application form for the 1934 Senior National A.A.U. Swimming Championships for Women to be held at the Olympic pool in River Rouge Park in Detroit, Michigan. She has printed her name as the entrant, signed above that, and then given her address as 1509 Ninth Ave. in Seattle, Washington. I grew up in Seattle and know that address is downtown, not far from the Washington Athletic Club, but quite a distance south by streetcar from the Greenwood district where my aunt grew up and where she attended high school. I wondered at first if this could be Ray Daughters' address given for convenience. But explaining the trek the swimmers made every day to the club, Doris Pieroth wrote that my aunt took the streetcar every day from "Greenwood at the north city limits, until she and her mother moved to a downtown apartment on 9th Avenue near Pine Street." Then Pieroth provides the last clue, "They [the swimmers] came from the homes of a single-parent dressmaker, a struggling entrepreneur with a small radio business, a financially ruined trucking company, and a musician." I see. Though unnamed, that single-parent dressmaker was my grandmother. Sometime between 1930 and 1934, the family split in all directions like the pool balls my grandfather racked time and again at his part-time job at Greenwood Billiards.

Olive sits before her open locker at the WAC. My father, her brother, an army private, stands guard duty in Hawaii. My grandfather rents a room in a boarding house on South Greenwood Ave. My uncle Don is nowhere to be seen. Broken, fragmented, Olive's family is rarely if ever mentioned in eight inches of scrapbooks. I remember being lost as a teenager. The ritual of suiting up for basketball practice helped, and the court was a place where I could step into an identity. Inside those boundaries and in that uniform, I was competent and valued. I was willing to work hard to keep the position and stats. I can imagine for my aunt the routine, the work, and the promise of swimming, measured in yards indoors and in meters outdoors, allowed her to work at such a self-concept and to insulate herself from the vagaries of her home life. This is who I am, she may have thought, an athlete, a world-record holder—with water as her "medium," her obituary would say seventy-two years later.

I wonder, though, about her inner life. What does she feel standing before her open locker where she hangs her wool coat, the cotton blouse and skirt her mother hand-sewed for her, and leather shoes and cotton stockings she exchanges for bare feet, a towel, a white bathing cap, and her black swimsuit with the winged WAC insignia on the front? Perhaps she folds the day's *Post Intelligencer* where her picture once again graces the sports page and sets the paper on the locker's shelf. Perhaps she looks in the mirror fastened to the inside of the locker's door and wonders what the world sees, not a surprising question for an eighteen-year-old girl, but one certainly complicated for her by reporters who search for language to define who she is and what she does. I'm sure she feels more comfortable in the water than out of it, where she must field all that talk and publicity. In water she has leverage. Poolside, on display, all that leverage drains away.

Looking back through her clippings, I find the world saw her as a "young bashful modest lass," "cheerful," "Smiling Olive," "lithe and graceful," a "pretty miss," sometimes "blonde" sometimes "brunette," who is "tall and youthful," "just a youngster but what a swimmer," one of the "four horsewomen" on the WAC relay team, at times "petite" and other times a "thoroughbred" and "powerfully built." She's "a regular girl and swell friend." She's a "Naiad," a "mermaid," a "natatator," and a "water shark" yet with "a feminine air." One of "Daughters' daughters" to begin with, she's a "Daughter of Neptune" in the end. In a July 1934 newspaper photo, she's on display in her swimsuit, propped like a starlet on the new Chevy to be awarded that evening to Ray Daughters. In a May 9, 1934, series of newspaper photos she's featured with three other women modeling the latest swimwear. The headline of one photo: "Park Board Stages Its Own Bathing Suit Parade," so that its members can "decide" how much (or how little) Seattle women could wear on the beaches. Another photo shows a man in a business suit kneeling next to my aunt with his tape measure running up her leg. The caption reads, "Although members of the Seattle Park Board sometimes believe theirs is a thankless job, Samuel Martin admitted there are times when it has its good points. While (left to right) Merna Merker, Dorothy Taft, and Mrs. Eddie Bauer stand by for inspection, he sees that the bathing swimsuit worn by Olive McKean, swimming champion is 'within the bounds of common decency' set down by the members of the board." Perhaps my aunt thought nothing of such a display. She is smiling in the next photo when Mr. Martin rejects the two-piece suit she models, a "bra" suit disqualified because it's far too revealing.

Seventy-eight years later, such a display is still eyebrow-raising news to me. But come on, what does a young boy think about his aunt when she's in her apron, kneading dough on the kitchen counter, or dressed in sweats with a stopwatch in one hand and a whistle around her neck, urging a swimmer to faster and faster times? He doesn't picture her as a pin-up girl. No, she was my dad's sister. Looking back through her clippings, I notice how many times she and other women swimmers are featured in their swimsuits, posing in line or on the starting blocks or seated on a diving board, hugging one knee. In an article titled "Icons of Liberty or Objects of Desire? American Women Olympians and the Politics of Consumption," Mark Dyreson explains that starting in the 1920s "American women were increasingly enmeshed in the process of making national identity through sport." The press stressed their attractiveness to convince an American public that such women were not to be feared politically. He concludes that these women athletes "were both symbols of new rights and powers, and sexual commodities who ranked alongside movie stars in American popular culture."

So perhaps my aunt's public saw her as an athletic sex symbol. It's more than I ever imagined. Through it all she seemed to maintain her sense of humor as well as modesty and grace—the price of popularity and athletic success she may have concluded and left it at that. When I wrote that first essay about my aunt's competing in the Olympics, I recalled our family's yearly visit south to Portland, where my aunt coached swimming and my uncle taught at Benson High School. I wrote, "Aunt Olive's hair was always short and frosted by the sun or chlorine. She wore no makeup, and her greetings were unadorned and genuine." Then from a boy's point of view I added, "I do remember thinking my aunt wasn't as pretty as my mother, but I knew she was tougher, an intense, single-minded coach who encouraged her own daughters to work at swimming until they became Olympic caliber themselves."

That's a sentence I wish to revise. My aunt surely took exception with the first half, and the more I study her scrapbooks, the more I agree with an April 26, 1934, *Gantner Swimming News* article that celebrates "brilliant new stars" on the swimming scene, one of whom was the "beautiful Olive McKean, of Seattle, who won the 100-yard championship for women." Yes, in photo after photo, from those early Green Lake shots of a fifteen-year-old to the young woman five years later celebrated by parades through downtown Seattle, or posing with Seattle notables, hockey players, airline pilots, and even the wife of a prominent sporting goods retailer, my aunt looks young and happy, and yes, beautiful. I see that now.

I imagine her standing years later in her sweat suit, clipboard in hand, ready for a session with the young women and men she coaches at the Multnomah Athletic Club. She closes her locker and twirls the dial as if to lock away the ephemera of renown, the transience of fame and beauty, the record of all that was accomplished long ago stored in files stacked in a box in a closet in the back room of a building in Florida—all that doesn't pertain to the moment at hand.

Abby Haight remembers my aunt in an *Oregonian* obituary, saying she "swam in Seattle's Green Lake as a child in the 1920s, was recruited by the nation's leading swim coach as a teenager and won a bronze medal at the 1936 Olympic Games—the 'Jesse Owens' Games' in Hitler's Berlin. Later, Mucha [my aunt's married name] was a swimming teacher, coach of champions and passionate organizer for national and international swimming events." One of my aunt's champions, Carolyn Wood, winner of a relay gold medal in the 1960 Olympics, said that "[s]he was very personal, consistent, kind and inclusive," and although the young swimmers knew Mucha was an Olympic medalist, she rarely spoke about that experience. I'm not surprised.

But don't let my aunt fool you. Like my father, her older brother, she was not prone to celebrate herself. Polite and deferential, she was easy to laugh and kind, though not without standards certainly, especially when it came to hard work, respect, and modesty—in effect, how one played the game. All our years growing up around her, my aunt never paraded her successes before us. Sitting in her living room, I explained how sorry I was that her Olympic medal had been stolen, or at least that's what I'd heard from my parents year after year. Then my aunt corrected me. Eighty-two and light on her feet, she got up, walked over to the mantle above her fireplace, rummaged in a candy dish, and then walked back to hand me a bronze coin a little over two inches in diameter. Cool to the touch, heavy, the bronze darkened, the obverse side read "XI OLYMPI-ADE, BERLIN, 1936" next to the figure of Nike. The reverse side displayed an Olympic champion carried in triumph by the crowd. That could have been Olive. Perhaps it was, her victory and the medal, like her scrapbooks, hidden in plain sight for the last sixty years.

Handwork

My grandmother, my father's mother, died in 1970. My memory of her has faded since then, though I do remember she had little to say to me, an inquisitive and untidy boy, about her history besides, "It's not for you to know." That reprimand still piques my curiosity. Occasionally, my cousins Judy and Jean tell stories about our grandmother's time as a cook in turn-of-the-century logging camps, her unusual friends, and the rumor that she sewed for the working girls. I've had little to add, until now that is, for I have discovered my grandmother's stitches, compositions assembled by hand on a sampling of linens and dish towels, her true cotton foolscap. A few years ago, my mother handed these things to me to give to our daughter, nostalgic keepsakes my mother may have thought, though I sense my grandmother would have said these pieces simply suggest busy hands, evidence that she was not an idle woman. I have them on loan. At first glance it's difficult to see any stitches at all, but when I turn the towels over, the sewing speaks up, hieroglyphs in handwork, stitches so small they might be analogous to whispers, the slightest mention of what held her world together *sotto voce*, the edges ironed and folded under and the stitches blind. I'm sure there's a story behind my grandmother's appliqué.

But one needs to be fluent in such a language, so I took my borrowed sack of hand-me-downs to a Jo-Ann Fabric store in Iowa City. The clerks, especially the older women, gathered around the measuring table and unfolded and straightened each towel, the apron, a baby's flannel pants, the dresser scarves. Then I wrote what they told me on lined paper and straight-pinned each sheet to its appropriate item—a pattern for what I wanted to say.

⊘   ⊘   ⊘

Items: Two old-fashioned dish towels made from kettle cloth or muslin, one with red piping down each side lengthwise and the other towel plain. Each measures 18 by 26 inches. If you fold one in half and then again in thirds, the middle third panel serves as frame and background for the design. On the plain towel, my grandmother tried to stop time in her kitchen, the center of her universe. She outlined a clock at the top of the frame, a pig tea cozy in the lower left corner, and salt and pepper shakers to the right.

But the clock centers her design. She loved cuckoo clocks. When we visited, my father would stop the pendulums so my little brother could sleep and wouldn't cuckoo in response all through the night. Her dish towel looks Norwegian with its bright red tulip in each corner, green leaves left and right forming a canopy above a clock for a kitchen warm and redolent with fried eggs and bacon, the stovetop piled with dishes and the basement door open. Down those stairs in the dark it sounds like she's looking for something gathered from her garden and home-canned. Glass clinking, something summer-ripened lies safe all winter beneath a clock that reads nine o'clock forever in black long stitch, each Roman numeral on the face discrete, the hours stored like mason jars on a shelf. On the backside of the cloth, however, my grandmother has sewn one hour to the next as if to concede that tulips wilt and peaches spoil and nothing lasts before the continuous thread of time.

The more colorful of the two, the towel with red piping exhibits a fruit motif. At first I assumed the basic geometric shapes, a kind of stylized collage, showed my grandmother's taste for art deco: a red apple nestles in a bunch of grapes below a chrome yellow apple from which a stem curves up through green leaves to support three perfectly round cherries—her cotton composition sewn together and decorated with white, light green, yellow, and red embroidery floss.

She has chosen fruit from the market and flowers from her garden, gathered Sunday morning, her harvest time, the back door open. I can see her wandering into her sunroom at the back of her kitchen, straw hat tied beneath her chin, her arms full of peonies and their attendant ants. They help open the flowers, she says, and shakes one ant from its bloom out the back door.

My cousin Jean doesn't remember our grandmother as especially religious or churchgoing, but Sundays did feel reverential at her house, especially when she turned on the radio for *American Radio Warblers*, thirty minutes of ten canaries, "the original feathered stars of the air," accompanied by organist Preston Sellers. When that opera started up, my grandmother's own canaries chimed in from cages around the sunroom. The house was full of bird music. The roller-rink pipe organ on the radio filled the spaces in between.

Sunday services for my grandmother meant tending her birds before indulging her own thoughts and handwork. Her birds were Harz Rollers, I read in the canary books, their songs a tour of bass and flutes and hollows, long vowels first rolled around an *r*. Then "oh Lulu oh Lulu what will you do, do, do." My grandmother refilled their seed trays. Poured water in the water tubes. Wired up new cuttlebone. She offered chickweed and spinach from her garden, a kind of bird eucharist, and stood back to watch her favorite canary sing to her, strut back and forth, jump to her hand and then her shoulder, a miniature yellow parishioner reflected in her glasses as she moved slowly, fruit basket in hand, to the dining room table.

The fruit arranged in a bowl, her birds quiet now, I imagine her sketching designs on pattern paper, then cutting out the shapes of leaves and shadows and folding the cotton twill under before ironing and pinning each shape onto the towel. Then she blind-stitches the edges, the needle pushed through the towel and back up to catch a few threads at the edge of a leaf or an apple and then back down through and up and so on. Holding the back of the towel close, I count sixteen stitches in an inch of the apple's edge—yes, sixteen "slip" stitches by hand. There are fourteen individual shapes, the two-toned apple at the bottom of the frame, the largest at four inches in diameter.

I very much wanted this composition, so painstakingly arranged and sewed, to speak to my grandmother's original thinking, how she imagined apples and grapes and cherries and then articulated them with pinking shears and a #10 crewel needle. When I asked the women at Jo-Ann Fabric about the composition, they said it looked like an Aunt Martha's iron-on pattern. Then one woman said, "See this dotted line along the edge of her apple. It's the pattern, and her sewing is just a little misaligned. That's all." I was disappointed, even a little embarrassed to be so naïve.

Then again, maybe I shouldn't have been surprised. I remember she had an LP of canary songs that she played off and on for her birds.

"Don't they know how to sing?" I asked her once.

"Yes, but not well. They listen to their betters and learn," was her answer, directed, I think in retrospect, to me.

What was I looking for in a dish towel? I remember my mother, on the occasion of a visit by her mother-in-law, hanging one of her framed paint-by-number old mill scenes on our living room wall. When I thought no one was watching, I dragged my mother's good living room chair to the wall and climbed up to look. My nose two inches from the canvas, I tried to find an errant brushstroke, a mistake to confirm my budding cynicism, or was it intimacy I was searching for? Then I lost myself for a moment in the brush marks, waves frozen on a hundred miniature seas, each contained within absolutely fixed and perfect shores. If I squinted, could I see my grandmother?

Apparently not, but she did see me. "I wouldn't do that if I were you," she said in a very firm voice. She must have heard my scooting the furniture and stepped from the guest bedroom into the hallway, her arms crossed and her expression icy. Sorry, I jumped down and dragged the chair back, guilty of climbing on my mother's furniture with my grass-stained tennis shoes. Or at least, I thought that was the charge. Thinking back now, maybe I was being warned against looking too closely, against faultfinding, warned to keep my feet on the ground, to keep my head down. "Get busy," her expression said, and we didn't speak of it again.

◊ ◊ ◊

Items: From my cousin Jean, photos of my grandmother circa 1910, each a surprise. In one she wears an elaborately embroidered dress with a lace collar falling to her waist, an outfit worthy of a Sunday outing from Walville, Washington, to Chehalis, twenty miles away by Stanley Steamer. In several others my grandmother poses with anonymous women friends. They hold hands in one photo, seated next to each other on porch steps, wearing identical full-length paisley dresses, their waist-length hair combed out. In

another she and a friend are seated in a field, both grinning as her friend tugs at my grandmother's skirt to reveal
stockings and high button shoes. It's girls' play, full of the
moment and teasing and laughter—a side of my grandmother unfamiliar to me.

My mother's photos of her some forty years later show
the modest woman I remember. In each my grandmother
wears a floral print dress buttoned to the neck—the same
nondescript design she sewed for Jean and Judy when they
were little girls—the requisite sweater, no jewelry, rimless
glasses, and her gray hair cut short and combed back at the
sides. Her mouth is always closed in these photos, though
if I hold a few just so, I suspect the makings of a smile, as
if she's remembering something indelicate or extravagant
in her past and satisfied that her careful demeanor and
self-composure will keep it there.

⌒   ⌒   ⌒

Item: A white cotton tea towel decorated with two cross-
stitch, comic dachshunds, one pink and one blue. Their
ears, backs, and tails are shaded in black cross-stitch. Each
has a tacked-on rhinestone eye. The pink dog smells blue
backstitch flowers, and the blue dog does the same for the
pink. Gold foil long-stitch leashes lead up and out into the
ether, where my grandmother might have chuckled, stitch
after stitch, for allowing herself such an upper-crust pre-
tension. Never a dachshund in a logging camp. Never such
a walk on Saturday afternoon with gold leashes. That's
what her friends Millie and Dorothy might have said
when they visited every spring, Millie the one-woman-
band vaudeville act, a fifth of rye packed in her bass drum.
Did they toast themselves and their independent lives? Or
did they raise their glasses to Dorothy, who regaled my
grandmother with tales of brutal work and hungry men in

Walville? These women cleaned for a living. They cooked. They sewed quick-release dresses for the "fancy ladies" who paid in admiration and cash, the mud in the streets deep enough to soil the finest hems and swallow the most agile of dachshunds.

✿ ✿ ✿

Items: Four oddly colored dresser scarves and an apron, all woven on my grandmother's loom as intricate as a giant cat's cradle, its raddle and reeds, its bobbin and frames, its foot pedals to split the warp so the shuttle could lay the woof back and forth back and forth, clacking. She rode that loom like a bicycle stationed between two cuckoo clocks, one at each end of her living room.

The women at Jo-Ann Fabric admired the consistent tension and even selvage of my grandmother's craft, but I didn't ask them about the colors and they didn't volunteer. One scarf is pale pink, for example, with a darker pink and lime-green pattern at the borders. I knew my grandmother had cataracts late in her life, but I'm not sure that explains the muddy brown and faded Chevy blue-green, the refrain of horizontal lime or mustard patterns when my father opened the gift from his mother each Christmas morning and thanked her, holding up another hand-woven tie that I never saw him wear.

✿ ✿ ✿

Item: One hand-crocheted afghan, approximately five feet by four and half feet, made of 180 granny squares, each four inches on a side. The pattern is number 55 in the *99 Granny Squares to Crochet* book one of the Jo-Ann clerks fetched to show me. The design looks like a flower with four center petals surrounded by eight, then twelve, then sixteen petals adjusted at last to form the square. My grandmother managed seven yarn color changes, as well, in each square. She must have used every leftover scrap of yarn she had, the hues circling the color wheel. The afghan looks motley, warm and cool, bright and muted at the same time. For a moment, I think that by choosing all the colors, my grandmother avoided committing to one, thus concealing herself behind the afghan rather than standing in front of it.

My wife, a bookbinder, said her grandmother taught her to crochet granny squares. "It's not too difficult. The skill comes in keeping the tension even so the squares come out the same size, like your grandmother's. See, four inches exactly." I turned this over in my mind: a no-pattern color collage and one size, again and again. Were I to fault this, Soetsu Yanagi, author of *The Unknown Craftsman: A Japanese Insight into Beauty* (one of my wife's book-binding resources), would reply, "Utility does not permit unsoundness or frailty . . . . Utility demands faithfulness in objects; it does not condone human self-indulgence. In creating an object intended for practical use, the maker does not push himself to the foreground or even, for that matter, to the surface. With such objects, self-assertion and error—if present at all—are reduced to a minimum. This may be one reason why useful goods are beauti-ful." Soetsu Yanagi could be describing my grandmother, whose story seems mute beneath her fastidious hand-work. Maybe I'll never find out whatever it is I'm not supposed to know.

On the other hand, maybe my grandmother is right in front of me all along, defined by such careful routines, her hands automatic as she watched something evolve stitch by stitch, a pot holder, a tea towel, an afghan, the colors going solid when I hold the afghan close and squint. The women at Jo-Ann Fabric seemed to understand as they refolded the towels and scarves and afghan and patted them together in the middle of their measuring table. "These are lovely things," one woman said in a hushed tone, paying homage, I imagine, to her own mother and grandmother. I see that now. Just as I understand the irrelevance of my last question. "How many stitches in the whole afghan, do you think?" It was an antsy kid question, a kid bored with homework or chores, his mind on baseball, but mesmerized by the work that went into three pounds of afghan.

One woman, an older clerk who has stayed through all my questions, counted under her breath one square for a few moments, and finally told me, "It's hard to say, but I'd guess maybe 3,200 stitches in a square." With 180 squares in the afghan, that adds up to 576,000 stitches, not counting the three rows of crocheted border and all the stitches that held the squares, the whole afghan, together. Over half a million stitches, by hand. With a single crochet hook.

"I bet my grandmother couldn't wait to finish this project," I said to the woman who refolded the afghan.

"Oh, no," the woman said. "It probably went by quickly. As good as she was. It's only when it was done, when her hands were still, that the sadness set in."

Sadness? I slipped the afghan back into my paper sack. How did I miss sadness? Although sketchy, our family stories about my grandmother suggest a difficult life but a heroic one: Raised by an aunt in Massachusetts and denied schooling, she left to make her fortune out West, married a mill worker, had three children, suffered through the Depression, a failed business with its cigar box of worthless checks, and a broken marriage. She lived the last forty-nine years of her life first as a single mom and then alone, working as a garment cutter, that is, when she wasn't riding a Greyhound bus south with a change of clothes and a Brownie camera, provisions enough for her impromptu vacation—a postcard from Guadalajara to my parents the first they heard of it.

I never suspected sorrow. Maybe kids don't. All appetite growing up, I remember my grandmother's solid demeanor and kitchen industry, her butter cookies every Christmas, her carrot pudding and hard sauce, an odd name for sugar, as if my grandmother's sweetness was difficult to come by. Hard sauce just tasted sweet to me. My cousin Jean, who lived with our grandmother for a time, recalls a story our grandmother told her about being deceived by a phony lumber baron visiting the East Coast in search of a debutante bride, how our grandmother followed him out West only to be abandoned, how she learned to fend for herself and her three children—my father, Jean's mother, and the youngest boy, always in trouble, the uncle our grandmother defended as "misunderstood." Such euphemisms. Such a Cinderella story gone bad, spun to console a frightened, adolescent girl.

"Did she take care of you?" I asked my cousin Jean. "What was she like?"

"She was kind," Jean said. "She had a beautiful carriage and deep blue-gray eyes. I felt safe with her. She would talk to me, explaining over and over about good manners and being gracious and standing tall."

☙ ☙ ☙

One last item: In this photograph, I'm three or four, born nine months after World War II, Cora Emilie Hibbard McKean's first grandson, posing in oxfords, white socks, custom shorts, a two-button tailored coat, and a grin beneath my tweed ivy cap. There is a right side and a wrong side to sewing, as any seamstress will tell you. Maybe it's the same with a story, "Not for you to know" less an injunction and more my grandmother's wish for me, a boy still happy in a three-piece suit, sewn by her in the hope that I too might stand tall and face my life with good manners and grace.

Crossover Toehold

My grandmother McKean loved professional wrestling. My father called it "wrasslin'." Grass stained from his own battles, my brother called it "bogus," but he and I watched nevertheless when our grandmother pushed a chair up to the black-and-white television in her living room on those Monday evenings we visited. She adjusted the rabbit ears as expertly as she plied her knitting needles, until the vertical hold held and the horizontal ring ropes tightened. What comes into focus in my mind is a man dressed in tails, carrying a hand-pump atomizer and ducking into the ring. A voice-over on the TV explains this is Thomas Ross, Gorgeous George's valet. Preparing for the grand entrance, Ross unrolls a small, cerise mat on the canvas and sets about spraying the ring with perfume, Chanel No. 10, as George was reported to have said, because why be half-safe with only No. 5?

My grandmother shakes her head at such rigmarole. I assume she'll root for the good guy tonight, Jesse James, a Greek who appears modest enough in his dark robe, a white towel wrapped around his neck. Tended by a "second" rather than a valet, James waits inconspicuously in the corner as trumpets blare suddenly off camera and the crowd starts to rumble and boo because here comes the flower himself, trumpets giving way to "Pomp and Circumstance" in tinny PA system violins. Casual and haughty,

Gorgeous George sashays toward the ring, sneering, chin uplifted as he peers down his nose at the crowd, ignoring the little old ladies with their hatpins and rolled-up programs. His left arm is hung with leis, which he tosses here and there into the crowd.

But it's George's bleached blond perm and incredible robe that stop my grandmother's knitting. Even in black and white, the robe is colorful. Such embroidery. Such quilting. So many sequins. What she knew about wrestling might be in question, but my grandmother certainly took the measure of extravagant clothing. She was a seamstress her whole working life, beginning in the logging town of Walville, Washington, in 1910, where she made dresses for the "fancy ladies." How they loved bows and ruffles, she might recall and how a chance at George's six-inch-wide, floor-length, gold lamé lapels and girdle and shoulder covering would have brought these girls running, cash in hand. How they would have sighed over the length of his purple silk robe with embroidered peacocks, a design Whistler might have chosen for a wallpaper to hide the rough-sawn walls of a patron's Victorian sitting room.

George's hair seems lit from within on this black-and-white screen, coifed by his hairdressers, Frank and Joseph, and held by Georgie pins, the gold-plated bobby pins he'd throw into the crowd, not enthusiastically but with a casual disdain as if he were simply looking to discard them equitably. Watching over my grandmother's shoulder, I imagine a Georgie pin whizzing by my ear and wonder about her irrepressible enthusiasm for and belief in professional wrestling.

"Get your filthy hands off me," George barks at the referee, who tries to give George the precursory prebout pat down. The crowd howls. The ring announcer pulls a mic down from the sky and explains that this is the main event, best two out of three falls, one-hour time limit. He introduces Jesse James from the great state of Texas, and then from Los Angeles, the "Toast of the Town, the Human Orchid, Gorgeous George." By this time, Thomas Ross has helped George out of his robe, the lining glittering gold beneath the house lights. George submits to the search—as long as the referee's hands are sprayed with disinfectant— the seconds depart, the bell clangs, and the television announcer says, "That's the end of George's pretty hair." When the two wrestlers lock up, my grandmother settles in to watch the bout, her knitting needles restarted.

Every time we'd visit, my brother would say, "How can you watch this, Grandma, it's fake." I tended to agree but kept quiet because our grandmother would shush us and move even closer to the TV. This evening George has taken the first fall over Jesse James, the holds undoubtedly illegal, George's famous credo being "Win if you can, lose if you must, but always cheat." George was the heel of heels, the villain in a melodrama that kept my grandmother rapt.

⊘   ⊘   ⊘

Her infatuation with wrestling has puzzled me for years. That is, until I took my seat in row 5 on the floor in the Peoria Civic Center, a two-and-a-half-hour drive from my home in Iowa City. This is the closest World Wrestling Entertainment match I could locate. I have come to put my skepticism to the test, and to find out why my proper, reserved, modest, self-contained, and conservative grandmother watched pro wrestling. In front of me, the ring sits empty. The crowd is restless. The line to the beer cart winds around the corner. I drift back to my childhood summers in Seattle when the carnival would set up in North City. I couldn't wait for the colors and lights and the smoke-filled air. Early in the morning, I'd sneak onto the grounds and lift a tent's corner to watch the carnies unpacking prizes inside the ring-toss booth. Next to it, the shooting gallery smelled like gun oil and fireworks, the .22 rifles laid out along the counter and a line of painted metal animal targets ready.

When a vendor walks by selling cotton candy, I'm back in Peoria and realize I have no idea who is on the card tonight or what the order of events might be. I climb the stairs back to the first landing to buy the "Official Souvenir World Wrestling Entertainment Program 2010." The program's graphics flash as big and glossy as its rhetoric. "This is where drama cries out for victory. This is where action bursts out of the gates. This is where the battle of epic proportions creates new heroes." The cover features the wrestlers Triple H and Undertaker standing behind John Cena, a movie star and the main draw, with his own action figure advertised on page two, complete with display stand. Around the cover's edge, a variety of wrestlers fly, dropkick, grimace, scowl, taunt, elbow smash, and raise their arms in victory.

It promises a loud and action-filled evening, more intense perhaps than the grainy black-and-white event on my grandmother's TV, my brother in the background grousing. But I didn't interrupt her concentration, and she never discussed the matches. I wish I had thought to ask her if the language of wrestling reminded her of sewing: The crossface chinlock, the camel clutch, the Rivera cloverleaf, and the inverted figure four, all could well be stitches. Of course, somebody always gets pinned in the end. Or maybe my grandmother imagined a new wrestling hero, whose secret holds—the buttonhole, the overcast, the blind stitch—would tie the ne'er-do-well into knots. Knocked flat, her villains would never see what hooked them from behind. Maybe in my grandmother's eyes, pro wrestling's "epic battles" simply ironed out life's ambiguities, the stakes and the players clear. What was good, righteous, ideal, and clean had a chance against evil, the nefarious world and its grime.

❧   ❧   ❧

The house lights blink. The crowd hurries. Over the PA, the WWE anthem "Hunt You Down" starts up. A thousand different faces mill and gather and find their seats. Cameras. Drinks, popcorn, casual dress, jeans, shorts, sunglasses propped on the tops of heads, hair tied back, ball caps. Many young men and women. Many with kids. I wonder if I'll spot my grandmother. Maybe her facsimile. But Jennifer shows up instead, pushing two kids ahead of her toward the seats next to me. I'm seated on the end of row 5, my single ticket in hand. In her middle thirties perhaps, Jennifer is Midwest friendly, round with glasses and short blond hair. Her son's name is Jarrett and his best friend is Nick. They are both ten and both wear orange "Never Give Up" WWE T-shirts. Nick clutches a foam "OK" big hand sign, and Jarrett wears orange WWE wristbands. In the picture I take, he looks just like his mother. He is also my fact source for the evening, having been a student of the WWE longer than I've known it existed.

Lights down. The announcer calls everything to order as the music ramps up, and from backstage sprints principal number one in our first match. Jarrett tells me he's Zack Ryder, and I find him in the program. At six foot one and 214 pounds, he's not really big, maybe a football safety's size. And I hope he's fast because plowing down the runway toward the ring is a man who looks as wide as a thunderhead. He's six foot one but weighs 392 pounds. It's Mark Henry from Silsbee, Texas, in a red singlet, his hair in cornrows and his foot-wide grin in the program infectious. But he's not grinning in the ring. After the bell, Zack Ryder gets on his trolley. The bad guy is a "heel," Jarret tells me, and the good guy is the "face," but I don't know who is who in this match, and when Mark Henry finally catches Zack, he squashes him—match over.

In the next bout the heel is obvious, for that evening the WWE has designated anybody or anything from the United Kingdom worthy of disdain. This bout features William Regal—six foot two, 240 pounds—from Blackpool, England. The crowd boos and taunts when he steps through the ropes, dressed in a black brocaded Elizabethan jacket embroidered with faux jewels and fleur-de-lys. He swaggers with aristocratic privilege, his straight blond hair Beatle length and his smirk lifted on one side in contempt for the crowd as he circles the ring. I'm sure he has the moral character of the sheriff of Nottingham. At once such conclusions headlock me into the narrative, the coming battle presenting only two choices. Hero or chump? Moral uncertainty or right and wrong? Existential angst or melodrama? It's easy. Presenting the Great Khalid, an East Indian who looms bigger each step he takes toward the ring until all seven feet three inches and 420 pounds of him ducks through the ropes. My opinion of him grows as he stands straight up, arms reaching into the lights as if to proclaim the Indian people's contempt of the Raj. I help make our case: Centuries of imperialism? An oppressive English aristocracy and military? What about American history? Didn't we throw the bums out as well? Isn't William Regal simply an emissary of King George? Yes, yes, the crowd chants. Suddenly I'm rooting for the American colonies, though my logic has wandered into the wilderness. I don't care. When the bell sounds, I'm on the righteous side.

◊　◊　◊

These battles, the writer George Felton claims, are not "needlessly complicated by storyline." In his essay,

"Wrestling with Myself," he says, "Wrestling may be a hybrid genre—the epic poem meets Marvel Comics via the soap opera—but its themes, with their medieval tone, could hardly be simpler: warrior kings doing battle after battle to see who is worthy, women pushed almost to the edges of the landscape." Again, I imagine my grandmother sitting back in her chair as the warrior Jesse James ducks under an elbow smash by Gorgeous George, grabs a handful of blond hair and George's arm, and whips him into the ropes that bounce him back and over the squatting James, who flips George onto his back, pulls his legs up and over, and holds on, George's feet bicycling the air. The referee slaps the mat one, two, three. Fall number two to Jesse James. Staggering around the ring, his hair disheveled, Gorgeous George grimaces in pain; my grandmother adjusts the skein in her lap and buttons her sweater as if the world has just righted itself and perhaps she should do the same.

At ringside in Peoria, George Felton's comment about women being pushed to the side would be loudly challenged by the WWE women wrestlers. As soon as the Great Khalid strides away from the ring, and William Regal bruised and vanquished, limps back to England, Alicia Fox and Eve arrive, athletically and dramatically, at center stage. Each is five eight or nine, not tall, not short, not model thin, but not heavy certainly—solid, strong, and acrobatic. Alicia is dressed in orange—halter top, shorts, black high-top boots, and orange knee guards—and Eve the same, except all in robin's egg blue. These are ensembles I can imagine my grandmother sewing as well as critiquing. I'm sure she wouldn't approve of such revealing costumes on young women in such a profession, but then again her own daughter, my Aunt Olive, was a world-class athlete and these two women in Peoria move with similar skill, grace, and independence.

Each has long, well-tended hair. An obvious detriment, too easy to grab, but the least of their worries, I'll discover, in the match to come. After the requisite strutting around the ring, Alicia holding up her championship belt—though it seems as if everyone that evening has such a belt—the two circle, crouch, then lock up at the bell. "Get her," the crowd yells. Suddenly I'm not sure who is doing what to whom, each woman quick and acrobatic, hair flying when not pulled. There are chokeholds, arm bars, and forward flips, Alicia leaping from the top ropes. Nothing stalls in this match and there's little posing or preening. If anything, the two dance through their routine, flipping each other, landing knee and forearm to neck, choking and whirling and jumping from the ropes and somersaulting, the mat resounding with each bump. I try to take a picture, but the house lights are down and the spots focus on the ring. My camera's shutter speed slows so each frame suggests an expressionistic blur of color and brushstrokes. This is what the match feels like, comets in chestnut brown and dishwater blond above an azure and orange stutter—feathers in a wing outstretched, white ropes scribing horizontal frames left and right, with one ring post bifurcating the shot. Alicia and Eve could be acrobats or trapeze artists in Cirque du Soleil, women who walk on their hands or climb a rope or swing trapeze bar to trapeze bar, but here in the ring they are swinging each other by the hair. Strong, agile, fearless, these women can handle themselves in a cheating world. This my grandmother would admire.

Looking at my own photographs of all the matches in Peoria, I think of George Bellows's painting *Stag at Sharkey's*. The exaggerated lines of the painting show the power in the legs, backs, and arms as the boxers pile into each other, their bodies bright under the ring lights but their faces obscured, one by a forearm and elbow, and the other because his head is bowed in a head butt. Outside the ring, an anonymous crowd stares from darkness. A few faces are illuminated at ringside: one fan, straw hat tilted back, looks up almost in reverence, a red-faced man wheezes in his tuxedo, a cigar-chomping man in the foreground turns toward us and gestures with his right hand toward the ring, the fighters locked in fury and the referee unable to break their clinch. The painting draws us into blood sport, the lust for a junior-high nosebleed, a contest designed to inflict real pain, to beat someone until we witness—and wish we hadn't—something like the sad killing of Benny "the Kid" Paret.

When I look at my Peoria photos more closely, however, the upturned faces at ringside seem ecstatic and bright beneath the ring lights. One woman grins in amazement and wonder, drawn in by the battle, the plot line given, the players chewing the scenery, and the stakes as simple as the welfare of mom and apple pie. George Felton calls wrestling "low rent Show Biz, this admixture of the asylum and the circus," and goes on to say, "Its emotional *reductio ad absurdum* taps my anger like a release valve, but its silliness allows me to feel superior . . . dumb and intelligent, angry and amused, on all fours yet ironically detached at the same time." Belief suspended and totally engaged, the crowd in Peoria cheers and jeers each bout until the main event. This grand finale introduces the worst the United Kingdom can offer, a six foot six, 270-pound Irishman named Seamus. His cropped, red hair and goatee stand straight up and out, undoubtedly a projection of his attitude. He saunters around the ring, his championship belt flung over his shoulder. He yells insults, pointing at the crowd.

Jarrett tugs at my sleeve and points at the corner of the ring and says that's John Cena. I see a clean-cut all-American kid wearing sneakers, cut-off jeans, a sweatshirt, and an orange WWE ball cap. Even though he's six foot one and weighs 240, he seems inconspicuous, waiting quietly in the corner as the announcer explains that this will be a Lumberjack match. Suddenly all the wrestlers in the WWE stable in Peoria, Illinois, march out of the dressing room and encircle the ring, the point being that anyone thrown out of the ring, Seamus or John Cena in particular, will be thrown back in by these gatekeepers.

Simple in theory, the whole match moves immediately from opening bell to chaos. Cena and Seamus roll and tumble. Outside the ring the watchdogs—Chris Jericho, CM Punk, Batista, The Miz, John Morrison, Rey Mysterio, MVP, Christian, Mark Henry, Jack Swagger, the Great Khalid, R-Truth, Matt Hardy, Cody Rhodes, Tyson Kidd, Evan Bourne, Dolph Ziggler, and The Undertaker—grimace and growl and haunt the ropes like specters swiping at the air. They toss Seamus back in, with a few elbow shots for emphasis. Two grab John Cena by the throat and try to drag him out, but he manages to pull both of his nemeses back into the ring. The rest of the troupe follows. It's silly and loud, but I'm on my feet. So is Jarrett, who at this moment looks exactly like a miniature John Cena, baggy shorts, sweatshirt, and armbands notwithstanding.

Quiet and attentive the whole evening, Jennifer, a pleasant mom, climbs up on her chair and screams, "Kill 'em!" No mistake. She's rooting for John Cena. Yes, yes, John Cena is fighting for us all. Caught up, I dodge and weave closer to see. Where's the National Guard when you need them? Where's the police, I think, my camera clicking away, but then as soon as I'm on my toes, a bell sounds, the house lights come up, and this choreographed riot comes to an end, with all the wrestlers standing in the ring taking a bow. Not a nightstick wielded. Not a tear gas canister thrown. When the villains and heroes parade out of the auditorium, waving, I'm still rebooting my worldview, gathering my wits, my coat, my ticket stub and program. I have no idea who won what.

Jarrett says, "Neat, huh?" and works his way over to John Cena for an autograph. Climbing down from her chair and back into an ambiguous world, Jennifer says nice to meet you. Yes, thank you for the picture and thank Jarrett for his help, I say, as I pack up, ears ringing, and aim for the quiet and uncontested night air.

❧ ❧ ❧

Three quarters of the way through the bout, Jesse James has trapped Gorgeous George in a full Indian death lock, a complicated submission hold. It looks painful. George writhes on his back, his legs twisted around Jesse James's left leg like a pretzel. George's right ankle is locked behind his own left ankle, which is trapped by Jesse's leg. The TV announcer Dick Lane proclaims George's hair a kitchen mop now and chuckles. After administering a few forearm shivers to George's head, James flexes and balls his fist and yells at The Human Orchid to give up. Such well-deserved humiliation. The crowd senses the match-winning fall at hand, their belief in righteousness close to vindication. Hand raised to count, the referee drops to his knees to spot George's shoulders on the mat. My grandmother stops knitting for a moment, frowning slightly as she watches and then reaches to turn the sound up. I can't tell if she's with the crowd or not. Will this be vindication for her as well? Is Jesse James really her champion?

Given the withering nature of a full Indian death lock, made famous by Wahoo McDaniel, my grandmother might think James has won the match. On the other hand, she may sense some tragic overconfidence by Jesse James, some inattention when he leans over too far, oh no, to strike George just one more time. The Human Orchid, still leg-locked, grabs Jesse's hair with one hand, the back of his trunks with the other, and pulls him upside down toward the mat, Jesse's head tucked under and his shoulders flat on the canvas. One, two, three, the referee pounds the canvas.

The winner, Gorgeous George! At this my grandmother goes humph. My brother throws his hands up, crying foul and fake. My grandmother turns the TV off, returns to her knitting, and nods. She seems resigned, even content. Remarkable! I was sure my very proper grandmother would champion the virtuous and the good, and therefore rue Jesse's loss, her hero vanquished by Gorgeous George, the villain, the foppish heel. But maybe George's victory is what she expected, even admired for its outlandish style. Perhaps such theater confirms my grandmother's view of the world and explains why she watches.

Wrestling as good versus evil? Wrestling as spectacle, where my grandmother can feel "angry and amused" at the same time, where she can hold contrary opinions in a kind of metaphorical double standard, her heroes virtuous but her villains entertaining and useful? "Always cheat," George says. In a just world, one would wish otherwise. Wrestling as a stage, where events unfold despite what we wish for?

Where does wishing get you? my grandmother would undoubtedly ask. In the real world, one does what one needs to do, even if it's sewing dresses for the "fancy ladies" from Walville to Seattle, who paid her in cash, who circumvented the rules and lived for the moment, who made an art of their own masquerades, the loggers' muddy boots left at the door and after the bell, their wages left on the bedside table. My grandmother knew these women and listened to them explain what it takes to survive. Jesse James, the hero in all his goodness, remains abstract, ambiguous in his nondescript robe, ducking out of the ring. But Gorgeous George flowers and preens and struts center stage. What a display! For a moment, my grandmother's attention seems fixed on his exotic cape and embroidered robe.

Perhaps she wonders where George's mother-in-law, a fine seamstress herself, found the material for such outfits, each more elaborate and outrageous than the last. Why not? The crowd keeps coming back. There's no perfect world, but there are ways to keep winning.

Caravan

As if imagination were lifting the dark, my eyes adjust. A reading lamp shines over a single bed. My grandmother, Cora McKean, comes into focus, propped up on pillows and tucked beneath a multicolored afghan she had undoubtedly crocheted.

Her trailer feels warm, my very presence compressing the air. There are letters and postcards and prescriptions on the nightstand. Peelings in a dish fill the medicinal air in her trailer with the scent of orange. A small sink holds a few dishes, and rosemary spills from a clay pot in one corner of her trailer. My grandmother looks pale, her gray hair thin, but her voice is steady when she says hello and tells me to find a place to sit. All six foot nine of me, bent over for the low ceiling, folds into a chair beside the bed. I wonder if I should embrace her, but I take her hand instead.

○ ○ ○

"Don't let on," my uncle told me as he led me toward his back door, that early February evening in 1970. I had driven 220 miles from Pasco, Washington, to Portland, Oregon, to see my grandmother, my father's mother. She was very ill. My father called me to let me know, and I called my uncle Don, my father's younger brother, to ask if I might visit. My aunt Nancy answered the front door and led me into their living room, where my uncle invited me to sit a moment, one lamp next to the couch barely lighting the room, the rest of the house dark and silent. This was unusual. My uncle, an electrician, who had hand built and played an electric organ, who assembled the first component stereo set I'd ever seen, filled his house with conversation and music during those visits I remember as a kid.

"Mom has her own trailer in our backyard," Uncle Don said into the quiet. I puzzled a moment. Why had my aunt and uncle left his mother to a trailer? Wouldn't her care be easier inside the house? Or maybe this had been her choice, her way to remain separate and close at the same time. After all, for as long as I could remember, she had lived by herself in a bungalow on the south side of Portland. She had supported herself as a garment cutter, tended her vegetable garden and flowerbeds, and remained stubbornly independent despite her advancing age and cataracts and a broken hip. "The cancer is inoperable," my uncle said. "We don't know how much time she has. Please don't tell her. She's looking forward to seeing you."

Shown into a crisp, moonless evening, the back door closed behind me, I stood alone on my uncle's back porch. A power cable ran from the house to her trailer parked up ahead, a light on in the window. My grandmother was eighty-four. I was twenty-four and anxious.

◌   ◌   ◌

Now I wonder about our last conversation, as fumbling as I was then. How ironic that she was living out the end of her life in a caravan, as if to prepare for her next journey wherever it would take her. How typical of my family that my uncle would ask me to keep the news of her cancer to myself. My grandmother certainly kept her own counsel.

Growing up, I was too intimidated or self-absorbed to ask her much of anything. I kept my distance, stayed polite, and watched my grandmother in silence. I was intrigued very young, by her adding "r" to words, her pronouncing "idea" as "ī-dē-er." What did that mean? Who was she and where did she come from? I repeated "ī-dē-er" under my breath down the hallway until my mother shushed me, afraid that I would offend my grandmother. Peeking around a corner, I saw her push Kleenex up her sleeve. Her hair was gray, and still cut short and brushed back at the sides. In the few photos I have of her, she faces the camera, her expression the same in each, a stern level gaze, her mouth closed, set. I imagine she might give a beat cop such an expression as he wrote her out a ticket for jaywalking, an injustice she would dignify with nothing more than her stone-faced silence.

As far as I knew, my grandmother never had a car, never drove. She understood the streetcars in Seattle, instructing my father which seat to take when he rode downtown to bring lunch to his father, my grandfather, who sold cigars in a tobacco shop on First Avenue. She would tell my father to set the basket by his feet so it would stay warm by the trolley's exhaust pipe under the floorboard.

Laughing, my father would tell this story after a few drinks before the Christmas dinners my mother assembled. Those years my grandmother spent the holidays with us, she would provide a box of her home-baked cookies: rosettes, rum balls, thumb-print cookies, Mexican wedding cakes, macaroons, snickerdoodles, fudge, and raspberry squares. She packed each type of cookie in a separate compartment and dusted them with powdered sugar. What an incredible amount of work and attention to order and detail she gave those cookies, but they were simply a sensory overdose when I was eleven or twelve, my dad's age when he rode the trolleys of Seattle in 1925 or '26.

My father's birth certificate says he was born in Chehalis, Washington, on June 4, 1914. His father, Charles
McKean, was a foreman in a Chehalis logging mill until
he fell off a ladder, broke his leg, and subsequently had
to have it amputated below the knee. My father's father
had been born in Lewiston, Pennsylvania. My father's
mother, my grandmother, was born in Somerset, Vermont, in 1886.

My mother always thought that her mother-in-law
had been adopted or taken in by two aunts who lived in
Boston. The 1900 U.S. Census lists Cora Emilie Hibbard,
fourteen, residing in Franklin, Massachusetts, and attend-
ing high school. Described as a "niece," she lives with her
brother Charles, ten, in the household of Lerna B. Cutis,
a fifty-nine-year-old female, and two cousins, Walter and
Catherine Cutis, both twice as old as Cora. My mother
remembers hearing that my grandmother was a good student and wanted to be a chemist, but her aunt refused to
sponsor her desire to attend Smith College, ninety-two
miles away in Northampton.

Franklin, Massachusetts, has a history of cotton mills
where women workers outnumbered men, an industry,
once dependent on cheap, slave-harvested cotton, that gave
way to woolen mills by the end of the nineteenth century.
Perhaps my grandmother tried to work, either in Franklin
or in Northampton's silk industry, famous for producing
sewing silk and embroidery thread. Working in the mills to
save enough money for college must have exhausted her.
She fell sick, upset as well by the lack of support from her
aunt, who resisted her charge's vision and likely considered such ambitions "unwomanly."

When my grandmother decided to leave Franklin for
good, I imagine the conversation with her aunt was brief,
without tears. Lerna Cutis may have spoken about the
futility of such schooling and suggested Cora needed to

think about marriage, adhering to the nineteenth-century notion of women as "moral guardians" and protectors of the home. What her aunt failed to recognize was Cora's desire and determination for self-sufficiency, that she was ready to strike out on her own. My grandmother, young and aware of the times, would think of herself as a "new woman," the phrase coined by the press at the turn of the century for a "supposedly young college educated [woman], active in sports, interested in pursuing a career, and looking for marriage based on equality."

Aspiring to go to Smith College, founded in 1875 and dedicated to educating "women of promise for lives of distinction," perhaps my grandmother felt like a "Woman for the World," if not through the offerings at Smith, then through her own pluck and initiative. I can see her tidying her room, her bags packed, a local newspaper folded open in her search for work and housing arrangements.

◈ ◈ ◈

I'm at a loss, however, as to why she bought a derringer and a one-way train ticket, passage first to Chicago, then St. Paul, and finally to the West Coast, a sixty-three-hour ride on the North Coast Limited.

Would she have composed a goodbye note to her brother Charles? Would she have mentioned the 1909 World's Fair in Seattle and her search for new opportunities? Settling into a second-class seat, four cars behind the steam locomotive working its way west, she writes a penny postcard to be mailed at a stop in Pennsylvania, far enough away from the outcry and criticism her disappearance must have generated. She has one suitcase, wears buttoned shoes, a long skirt, and a white blouse beneath her travel jacket. She has made her own hat, the long pins another safeguard. In her handbag, she keeps enough cash for tickets, maybe a sleeping compartment, for food at stations along the way, farther and farther apart as she watches, day after day, the country widen into plains and then rise up into the Rockies, the peaks snow covered and etching a sky so blue she shades her eyes and catches her breath, unused as she is to this new elevation's thin air.

It was an audacious escape for a single woman, my grandmother, at the turn of the twentieth century! Maybe she felt herself part of a larger reform movement, women in the Progressive Era insisting on their independence and equality even within marriage, their "personal liberation" through birth control, their opportunity to work outside the home and earn fair wages. How she must have held herself, anxious but clear-eyed and steady, her long hair neatly tied up, a collar fastened with a brooch, a young woman's face reflecting back from a coach window at dusk, the darkness closing in around her seat on the first night of her leaving.

Then again, her sudden departure was simply in character, such tight-lipped independence part of who she was. Back in the 1950s, our family would lose contact with her, only to discover that she had taken a ship to Hawaii or the Greyhound bus to Mexico for Spanish lessons. As a boy, I turned her postcards over and over, the stamps and postmarks exotic. Twelve years old and not a little envious, I imagined her wandering the beaches barefoot or climbing an Aztec ruin, beholden only to herself. Even now, I'm surprised by the risks she took venturing alone into unfamiliar territory, armed with guidebooks, intrigued by the plazas, the mariachis, the market stalls and their marigolds and chilies, their hand-dyed wool rugs, the cotton blouses cross stitched in red and green. But I realize that being alone was not unfamiliar to her, a woman in Guadalajara, the City of Roses, who understood intention and carriage were her best allies, moving through the world as if she knew exactly where she wanted to go. When she returned weeks later, my father drove to Portland to pick her up for the holidays. She'd sit in our living room and knit, without looking, her hands moving fast.

⊘ ⊘ ⊘

Her hand in mine is dry, nearly translucent but supple despite a life of tying knots. Knitting, weaving, crocheting, quilting, her forefinger and thumb holding the needle, and the thimble on her middle finger pushing the needle through the cloth, stitch after stitch. The years have gone by. She is smaller than I remember. I rearrange my knees in the tight space. Behind her rimless glasses, her eyes still flash pale blue, her cheek moist. She looks amused at my predicament, her mouth turned up as if she understands how difficult this is for me, this journey down the Columbia River to visit her.

⊘ ⊘ ⊘

Why my grandmother left Franklin, Massachusetts, in 1909 seems clear enough, but her journey to the southwestern corner of Washington State and her marriage to my grandfather remain as mysterious as her birthplace in Somerset, a town in southern Vermont, unincorporated in 1937. The 1910 Census for East Chehalis in Lewis County, Washington, lists Cora Hibbard as a single woman born in Vermont, working out of the home she rents and making dresses for a living. My cousin Judy says our grandmother once mentioned living in Walville, one of the ragtag frontier logging towns in southwest Washington State. She cleaned and cooked for the loggers. By the 1930s, Walville had disappeared, a victim of its own clear-cutting. For my grandmother, Chehalis, twenty miles away, must have felt like a step up, and by June 21, 1913, she had met and married Charles Clayton McKean, a foreman in the sawmill and one day, my grandfather.

I heard very little of this growing up. The older I get the more details I discover about my grandmother's story. My mother raised my brother and me in the "seen but not heard" philosophy of child rearing, and no one of my family, aside from my dad, volunteered to clarify the past.

Standing on my uncle's back porch, I wondered what to say to my grandmother. My cousin Judy had floated rumors that sparked my curiosity. Did our uncle Don really spend time in reform school? Did my great uncle Charles, my grandmother's brother, finally call from back east during the Great Depression to say he would like to come out west and visit her? Had she asked him if he had any money? With his answer, did she really say, "Don't come"? And then hang up? As a seamstress in Seattle, did she keep individual dress forms on hand for wealthy patrons who wired their orders from California? Did the Crash of '29 leave her with a cigar box full of bad checks and a family coming undone? After that, did she sew for the prostitutes on First Avenue in Seattle, customers who admired good clothing and paid in cash?

I wanted to ask about such clientele and how she survived the Depression, but this hardly seemed the time. As the light in her trailer window fluttered, all I could think about was something my brother had told me. In the summer of 1967, when I was twenty-one, our grandmother had stood in my parents' living room and watched me through the front window as I helped my friends load our D/Altered drag racer onto a trailer. "He's headed for trouble," she said under her breath, and my brother overheard her.

He told me later, "I said, 'No, Grandma. Jim's not driving that on the street. It's for the drag strip.' But you know that expression she'd get, just like Dad's." Yes, I remembered: Her head shaking a deliberate "no" back and forth. Mouth set. Eyebrows gathered, the muscles in her jaw flexing slightly.

"There's trouble there. He's headed for big trouble," she told my brother. Yes, trouble I'd survived, I thought, having driven all day to stand on my uncle's porch and wonder what I had to say for myself? I wanted to be deferential of course. Hesitant, unsure, maybe even shy, I walked ten paces forward, knocked once, and she asked me in.

◌ ◌ ◌

I'm still trying to find my place in her cramped trailer, my head even with the polished cupboards, the counters stacked with sewing and towels and half-finished knitting, needles stuck in skeins, the clutter of her industry around her. Could we discuss her sewing, her love of cuckoo clocks?

"How have you been?" I ask instead.

"Oh, you know," she says, and lifts her right hand as if to set the question aside, dismissing any secrets my uncle and I keep as irrelevant. "Would you hand me a Kleenex?"

And I do, glad to be useful. She removes her glasses and rubs her eyes. Her face is square and drawn by illness, her shoulders rounded beneath her housecoat from years of work over a loom or at a cutting table. I don't know what to say. She waits.

"I'm still playing basketball. Remember our visiting after the Far West Classic at Uncle Chuck's? You brought carrot pudding steamed in a coffee can."

What I don't say is that I was tired and sore and irritable then. We'd lost a game earlier that evening because I had missed the last shot.

"Have you put your experience to good use?"

The question surprises me, it's so direct.

I tell her about playing basketball for Washington State University, and afterward traveling to Italy to play basketball for a washing machine factory. Then I played for a team called the Gillette All-Stars that travelled across Europe. After the games, we handed out razor blades and pennants to the crowds. I tell her about my job as an English teacher and basketball coach at Columbia Basin College, lamenting my six-classes-a-quarter teaching load and recruiting for the basketball team and driving the dilapidated basketball van to the games.

"You're employed, aren't you?"

Both a statement and a question, but I hear no sympathy. None. Then I worry, am I confirming her view of me, a young man prone to trouble, racing at 125 miles per hour with no steering?

I live by myself, I tell her. I don't tell her I ride a 750 Honda motorcycle or that I indulge on weekends, the parties lasting into early morning. I tell her I have plans to travel to Mexico in the coming year. "To study, you know. I've always remembered your travels to Guadalajara."

She doesn't smile. Does she know I'm holding something back? "Your school should offer Spanish," she says as a corrective, pointing me toward something useful. "There are books as well. And records. It helps to prepare."

"Yes, I mean to study," I say, leaving her hand at her side.

Half in shadow, she looks away as if to contemplate something I cannot see, nods once, and turns back into the light, her chin dropping a little so she can see me over the top of her glasses.

Her gaze holds steady, as if to claim me for her own. She presses her palms together and then tugs the afghan up closer to her chest. At twenty-four years old, I'm unprepared, I realize, for my own future beyond her trailer door, unprepared to comprehend her story, unprepared for her leaving us all.

◊   ◊   ◊

Forty-six years later, I'm sitting at my desk, trying to rec-
ollect what else she may have told me or what she asked. I
think she understood what was at stake, lying there in her
warm trailer, and how precarious her future had always
been. When I said goodbye that evening, I understood less
about her past and more about my legacy as her grandson.
My uncle had asked that I take care, given her condition.
"Don't let on you know," he had said, but I knew she knew
already. And she sent me on my way.

Bound

Uncut this could be Whitman's hair, the grass on this gentle slope overlooking oak trees that mark the boundary of Hickory Hill Park. I remember the trails, the limestone foundation of a settler's house long abandoned, all the seasons of falling—leaves, then deep snow.

We could lie here, my love says, pointing to a number at the far corner of her map that has led us down a single-lane road to this back edge of Oakland Cemetery in Iowa City. We are in our fifties, our only daughter married a month ago and moved away, leaving a houseful of silence. And my love, who plans every day, would like a stone for our names and a marble bench for anyone who might stop here to sit and think a moment and watch—chin in hand— the morning breeze wash the leaves to gold. Such tidiness.

"What do you think?" she asks, kneeling to run her hand over the grass, the same way she smooths soil over seeds in her flowerbeds.

"Very peaceful." In the distance, beneath the oaks, a broken rail interrupts a fence edging the park. The trail, the way out, must lie beyond those trees, I imagine. She tugs at my sleeve. She looks inquisitive and earnest. I help her up.

"Would we face east or west?" she asks me.

I'd rather not face any way, I think to myself, but I don't know how to tell her this. And never have, really. These inclinations to order our life together I have so admired and loved about her for more than thirty years. "I have to go," I say sometimes, but I'm not sure where.

She's an artist of enclosures, an artist of the beautiful box. Such as our house, a story-and-a-half cottage built one hundred years ago, the front door locked. Inside we have restored woodwork and refinished raised panel doors. The floors are quarter sawn. The windows are double hung, framed in oak, and set with blinds, so my love can ration the light falling on our wool carpets, on her grandmother's ancient and recovered sofa, on our cherry wood table, paintings and watercolors and pictures, and a pendulum clock she winds once a week.

When I meander home after work and turn my key in the lock and drop my books and bags in the hallway and find her in the backyard, wand in hand above buckets of flowers, I love all over again the thought she gives to our space. We have brick paths and a cedar-fenced yard lined with arborvitae and the white pine she planted twenty years ago, branches soughing thirty feet up in the Iowa wind, the trunk a foot in diameter. There are heavy, fired-clay pots and beds tended and tidy, turned, mulched, and watered. She has organized the seasons to visit us, hyacinth and bearded iris and daffodils in the spring, shasta daisies and golden marguerites and rose mallow for summer, asters and marigolds and sedum into fall, and for all seasons the everblooming bleeding heart.

"Let's sit here," she says late summer afternoons, pointing to a deck chair next to the cedar trellis we prop up and tie to the railing with twine each year. Time slows. The ice makes my glass of tonic weep. I watch her clematis, that distant cousin of bindweed, turn its purple flowers toward the sun and inch and coil its way around the legs of my chair, up over the armrests, and take my arm like a shy lover.

✿ ✿ ✿

I need to go fishing. Wander where the stream wanders. My love would want to know for how long. An hour? How little she understands about this. I have tried to show her— floating the San Juan or hiking the River of the Lost Souls, and even once trolling for silvers in Icy Strait off Juneau, Alaska, where it was I who finally began to understand. When we visited Juneau's natural history museum, I was soon three displays ahead of her, admiring the economy of the Athabascan sleds, their thin runners and sinew ties. These hunter-gatherers carried everything with them— pemmican, a change of clothes, such fine stitches in animal skins to keep the water out, snares and tools, and small dolls for children wrapped in fur, an amulet changing its shape for luck or the gods—all stowed in the sled behind the dogs, stopping now in a place the Athabascans named for directions to the next. Standing there, rocking foot to foot, I imagined a camp before the setting sun named "Downstream for Red Salmon" or "Almost to Berries."

But when I looked back over my shoulder, I saw my love admiring the elaborate, full-sized replica of the Tlingit cedar house, a people who stayed put. They lived on good salmon and halibut from the sea. Using fire and axes, they hewed canoes from cedar logs. They wove blankets and carved raven and eagle and bear and turtle masks and stacked orca on salmon on bear beneath the watchman of their totems standing twenty feet high outside their houses.

I have read that each Tlingit is a member of a moiety, raven or eagle. That smaller units within are known as clans, and everyone's name is the property of a clan. A newborn receives the name of ancestors. No one's going anywhere. For each clan, "house" refers both to the physical structure and the matrilineage associated with the structure, and each house has a formal name. From where I stood, my love looked wide-eyed and ready to move in.

When I walked back to fetch her, she said, "Look at those bentwood boxes. I want one." She knew already how they were made, a single red cedar plank beveled or ker-fed at the inside corners and steamed so the plank went pliable enough to bend in three directions back onto itself to make the sides. A cedar top and bottom sealed the box. Made in all sizes, they served as simple storage or as small watertight canteens, or as cradles, or large and painted as someone's fragrant coffin. My love's a Tlingit at heart.

I shouldn't be surprised. Bookbinding is her art and craft. In a small carriage barn in our backyard, her studio holds nipping presses, board shears, machines with cast-iron bases, boxes to store rolls of leather and cloth, and flat files, their drawers full of binder's board and handmade papers. There are glue pots and iron weights and sharp knives and wet stones and spoke shaves and needles and cord and bone folder after bone folder. She has exercised her arts on me. She hands me small folios of paper that fit in my shirt pocket. For my "flights of fancy," she says, and I write what comes to mind, poems about the wind, the ailanthus that sheds all over our house, a weed emblem-atic of the wanderings of my mind, fragile and messy and named tree of heaven for its reaching. "Give them back to me when you're through, OK?" she says.

When I have enough, she stacks the folios in her sew-ing frame and sews through the folds with unbleached linen thread over tapes, each section stitched to the next. She sews head and foot bands, the silk thread lining up turn after turn. Then she makes a case—board, spine, then another board covered in cloth. She wraps the sewn pages in end sheets and pastes the book into its case and imag-ines the ailanthus in spring bloom, and cuts and pares dyed goatskin to wrap the spine of my book, green leather branches and leaves inlaid into the gray cloth cover like hands holding everything I have to say.

This is her work. Behind her bench, sleeves rolled, her apron marked "Reliure," she builds cases and airtight boxes, and repairs old books with wheat paste and Japanese kozo paper. She mends tears, stiffens spines, understands the grain, the verso and recto, the gutter and fold. She celebrates the margins. She stands invisible behind the text, her handiwork everywhere but nowhere to be seen in someone's cherished book, open late at night, the spine tight beneath his lamp and thoughts and wanderings.

This is why I watch her. Her beautiful enclosures tidy and brighten my life, so much so that I must not forget what's inside. Even the trash she wraps seems composed when I walk it outside to the bin. Even the cardboard boxes she packed one day after her basement cleaning were tied up fast with string. "Will you please take these to the Goodwill," she asked, "and get a receipt?"

"What are we giving them?"

"Odds and ends."

Oh, she means well, my love. But I made sure to untie the string and look first. No, I did not give my nesting pots to the Goodwill. Nor my white gas stove to the Salvation Army. Nor my ground cloth, rain fly, and tent stacks, though I have no tent. Nor my compass and trenching tool, tarp and twine, my backpack and canteen. Nor my halazone tablets and waterproof matches, my knives and sharpening stone—none of my symbolic gear for a wandering mind.

❧   ❧   ❧

"Number 27 and 28," she says, reading from the map of the Oakland Cemetery. I'm back from daydreaming, and rest my hand on her shoulder. She looks up at me, squinting for the sun. "What shall we do?" I knew this question was coming. I love her for thinking this way. How tidy. But I am loose-leaf. She is bound. One day she wishes to be dressed in silk and bound in oak boards and returned to the earth. I wish to be dust resting on her upturned hands and scattered in one breath.

"It seems so claustrophobic. I'd rather be left to the wind," I say. "Instead of 'Rest in Peace,' how about 'On His Way' or 'Gone after Chinook'?"

"Well, I want you with me," she says. "If not by my side, then swept up and held forever and ever in my arms."

Notes

Introduction

2: Robert Hayden, "Those Winter Sundays," in *Selected Poems* (New York: October House, 1966), 55.

3: Bret Lott, "Toward a Definition of Creative Nonfiction," in *Contemporary Creative Nonfiction: I & Eye*, ed. B. Minh Nguyen and Porter Shreve (New York: Pearson, 2005), 197.

3: Vivian Gornick, *The Situation and the Story* (New York: Farrar, Straus and Giroux, 2001), 13.

Lesson Plan

6: T. S. Eliot, "The Love Song of J. Alfred Prufrock," in *Collected Poems 1909–1962* (New York: Harcourt, Brace & World, 1963), 3–7.

Rootie Kazootie One-Man Band

15: Hayden, "Those Winter Sundays."

23: Robert Frost, "The Road Not Taken," in *The Poetry of Robert Frost*, ed. Edward Connery Lathem (New York: Henry Holt, 1969), 105.

28: William Stafford, "Judgments," in *Stories That Could Be True: New and Collected Poems* (New York: Harper & Row, 1977), 118.

28: Elizabeth Bishop, "Filling Station," in *Poems* (New York: Farrar, Straus and Giroux, 2011), 125.

Payoff

39: Dylan Thomas, "Fern Hill," in *Dylan Thomas: The Poems*, ed. Daniel Jones (London: J. M. Dent & Sons, 1971), 195.

Queen for a Day

55: Roger Cohen, "The Battle to Belong," *New York Times Sunday Review of Books*, Jan. 9, 2015.

57–58: Thomas, "Fern Hill."

Stations, 1979

73–74: Richard Wilbur, "Love Calls Us to the Things of This World," in *Collected Poems, 1943–2004* (Orlando, FL: Harcourt, 2004), 307.

Dyed-In-the-Wool

83–84: *Dunn County History* (Dallas: Taylor Publication Co., 1984), 244.

86: Ellen M. Plante, *Women at Home in Victorian America: A Social History* (New York: Facts on File, 1997), xi.

87: "Skinner v. Skinner," *Reports of Cases Argued and Determined in the Supreme Court of the State of Wisconsin*. Vol. 5 (Milwaukee: R. King & Company, 1854–96), 449–58.

87–88: "Johnson v. Johnson," *Reports of Cases Argued and Determined...* (Milwaukee: R. King & Company, 1854–96), vol. 4, 154–63.

88: Catherine B. Cleary, "Lavinia Goodell, First Woman Lawyer in Wisconsin," *Wisconsin Magazine of History* 74, no. 4 (Summer 1991): 260. See also Joseph A. Ranney, "'The Last Thing a Man Becomes Progressive About': Wisconsin Women and the Law, 1846–1920," in *Trusting Nothing to Providence: A History of Wisconsin's Legal System* (Madison: University of Wisconsin Law School, 1999), 203–25.

91: Catherine B. Cleary, "Married Women's Property Rights in Wisconsin, 1846–1872," *Wisconsin Magazine of History* (Winter 1994/95): 128.

92: Mark Twain, *Adventures of Huckleberry Finn*, ed. Charles Neider (New York: Doubleday & Co., 1985), 31.

Posting

97: W. H. Auden, "The Unknown Citizen," in *Selected Poems: Expanded Edition*, ed. Edward Mendelson (New York: Vintage International, 2016), 93.

98: Maxine Kumin, "Silver Snaffles," in *In Deep: Country Essays* (New York: Viking, 1987), 76.

98: Jane Smiley, *A Year at the Races: Reflections on Horses, Humans, Love, Money, and Luck* (New York: Knopf, 2004), 47.

101: E. B. White, "The Ring of Time," in *Essays of E. B. White* (New York: Harper & Row, 1977), 144.

So Much More

104, 108: A. E. Housman, "To An Athlete Dying Young," from Poetry Foundation (poetryfoundation.org).

110: Doris Pieroth, *Their Day in the Sun: Women of the 1932 Olympics* (Seattle: University of Washington Press, 1996), 2, 72.

111: David Eskenazi, "Wayback Machine: 'Queen' Helene Madison," *Sportspress Northwest*, April 19, 2011 (sportspressNW.com/2011/04/wayback-machine-queen-helene-madison/)

118–19: Doris Pieroth, "Toast of the Town in the Thirties: Seattle's Washington Athletic Club and Its Champion Swimmers," *Pacific Northwest Quarterly* 87, no. 1 (Winter 1995/96): 18, 21.

121: Mark Dyreson, "Icons of Liberty or Objects of Desire? American Women Olympians and the Politics of Consumption," *Journal of Contemporary History* 38, no. 3 (July 2003): 435, 458.

123: Abby Haight, "Olive McKean Mucha Obituary," *The Oregonian* (www.oregonlive.com/sports/oregonian/index.ssf?/base/sports/114438392544100.xml&coll=7).

Handwork

132: Soetsu Yanagi, *The Unknown Craftsman: A Japanese Insight into Beauty* (Tokyo: Kodansha International, 1989), 143.

Crossover Toehold

141–42: George Felton, "Wrestling with Myself," in *Mirror on America: Short Essays and Images from Popular Culture*, 2nd ed., ed. Joan T. Mims and Elizabeth M. Nollen (Boston: Bedford/St. Martins, 2003), 334.

143: See Robert Haywood, "George Bellows's *Stag at Sharkey's*: Boxing, Violence, and Male Identity," *Smithsonian Studies in American Art* 2, no. 2 (Spring 1988): 2–15.

144: Felton, "Wrestling," 335.

Caravan

153: "Introduction to Women in The Progressive Era," National Women's History Museum (https://www.nwhm.org/online-exhibits/progressiveera/introwomenprogressive.html).

153: See Smith College mission statement (Smith.edu).

155: Sophie Coonitz, *Marriage, a History: How Love Conquered Marriage* (New York: Penguin Books, 2005), 154.

About the Author

James McKean earned his MFA from the University of Iowa Writers' Workshop and his PhD from the University of Iowa. He has published three books of poems, *Headlong, Tree of Heaven*, and *We Are the Bus*; and a book of essays, *Home Stand: Growing Up in Sports*. A professor emeritus at Mount Mercy University in Cedar Rapids, Iowa, he still teaches for the Queens University low-residency MFA program in Charlotte, North Carolina.